There have been moments of conversations that have had huge resonance. And I don't know—I don't care— how I've applied them. Part of my practice is that I allow this to happen. I let things just sit in the back of my head and I don't work at them too much, because if you try to work at an idea or a feeling, you work it to death and it just disappears. But if it has that much resonance, it will come through somehow.

I'll look back in three years' time and ask 'what am I doing now that I hadn't planned to do before the project?'. Although things naturally evolve anyway, I do feel that this is a pathway perhaps to something different. I would like it to be. I would like to keep the group together.

The project was quite fragmented. Well, we were all very busy with a lot of other stuff (i.e. University commitments)… I never felt like I had a very pre-determined role other than I felt a responsibility to make sure it didn't turn into a public art project [laughs]. And that where there was a form for something that came out of our shared conversation, that I would help find that just because I'm used to perceiving where there's a form emerging in terms of there being an event or there being something visual.

There is a trial and error when it comes to formulating research questions and hypotheses—there is really thinking and conceptual planning based on what we know, we deduce this that leads us to this hypothesis that we will then answer by doing these manipulations. In that respect, I don't think the project has actually helped me.

The lack of goals has actually been really quite refreshing. The fact that we've had quite a few afternoons down at Furnace Park and there hasn't really been any end goal. It has been: 'let's just see how it goes,' and I don't think in Engineering or actually very much within life, you get to do that very often. Especially doing experimental work, you have to be very clear as to what your goals are. You often use expensive equipment, so you book in time on it, you have to be very clear what you're going to do in that time, and just to play and not know what you're doing isn't something we do... I'd like to make things a lot more open-ended but I think it's still difficult... For any funding we have to have very clear goals. [In future collaborative work] I think we're still going to have to have an end goal, a very particular event. But then I think that the process as to what we do will remain quite open.

'This is a jewel, this is a jewel,' but people don't want to see the jewel; they want to see the museum case and the little brass thing that says, you know: 'this is a jewel'.

I don't think we came up with any deep questions at the end of the day. I don't think we've solved a problem for liminal spaces in the city. But there's something quite radical in that we didn't do that, because it wasn't just by mistake. I think without the park we might've been scuppered and we might have come up with a sort of clever little idea of how our practices interweave. And it would've been okay, but the park sort of made us abandon our specific disciplines.

I want people to know about what we've done—letting people know how we worked together on quite an open project. That's why it's so different to what I've done before. It evolved as we've gone along, and I think we've managed to get a very good team working, which, you could really think that could be quite difficult; you've got people from such wide variety of backgrounds and disciplines. So I'd like people to know about that, and I think the book will be a good outcome, because people will be able to see some kind of creative process.

This book collects the writing, images and ideas that a group of artists and university researchers produced over a ten month exploration of each other's work as they explored a wasteland in Sheffield. The project was called Sandpit, which seemed right when we first entered the wasteland on a clear February morning. Along the way we lost that name and ended up elsewhere, still in the wasteland, but doing things that none of us had planned. More than anything this book catalogues that drift.

From the beginning, we designed a project where the artists were integral to the research and not added on at the end, to communicate the 'findings'. As a result, there is no collective arrival here, but rather a set of conclusions and critiques all stemming from the same process. Its interesting how diverse and personal these responses are when the project itself was performed collectively, even down to the writing of this book. Most of the authors are drawn from those who remained at the end of the collaboration: six university researchers (an engineer, a biochemical engineer, an ecologist, a materials scientist, a speech therapist, a folklorist) and two artists (Bob Levene and Hester Reeve). I've specified the artists' names because it somehow seems wrong to further 'specialise' them in the way which seems natural to researchers.

With such a diverse group, we began by working out connections between people. This wasn't always between researcher and artist but sometimes between researcher and researcher. By the end we were all trying to understand and apply artistic practice to the research process. The book has been designed to reflect and make sense of this. It will be useful to anyone interested in integrating artistic practice with other research disciplines. There are three sections to it. The first features essays from the participants, the second captures a group blog we did, the third provides the chronology of the project and documents speeches given at a delicious breakfast we held in the wasteland in which we sited most of our work. This wasteland is called Furnace Park, named after the 19th Century cementation furnace that overlooks it. The furnace ceased operations in 1951, the year of the first Miss World pageant, the first British residential tower block and the first computer to run a business application. Back then, a project such as this would be inconceivable. We hope you gain something from reading this book.

—Matthew Cheeseman

NO PICNIC

This edition published May 2014 by NATCECT
ISBN 978-0-907426-75-2

Print on demand version available from AND Publishing
ISBN 978-1-908452-43-6

Contributors
Alison Beck, Matthew Cheeseman, Caroline Evans, Bob Levene,
Jonathan Paragreen, Hester Reeve, Arne Schröder, Sarah Spencer

Project Co-ordinator
Matthew Cheeseman

Photography
Gemma Thorpe, Andy Brown and participants

Editorial and Design
HAND
ha-nd.com

Thank You
Amanda Crawley Jackson, Tim Lewis, The Milestone,
SKINN, Sandrine Soubes, Tom Stafford

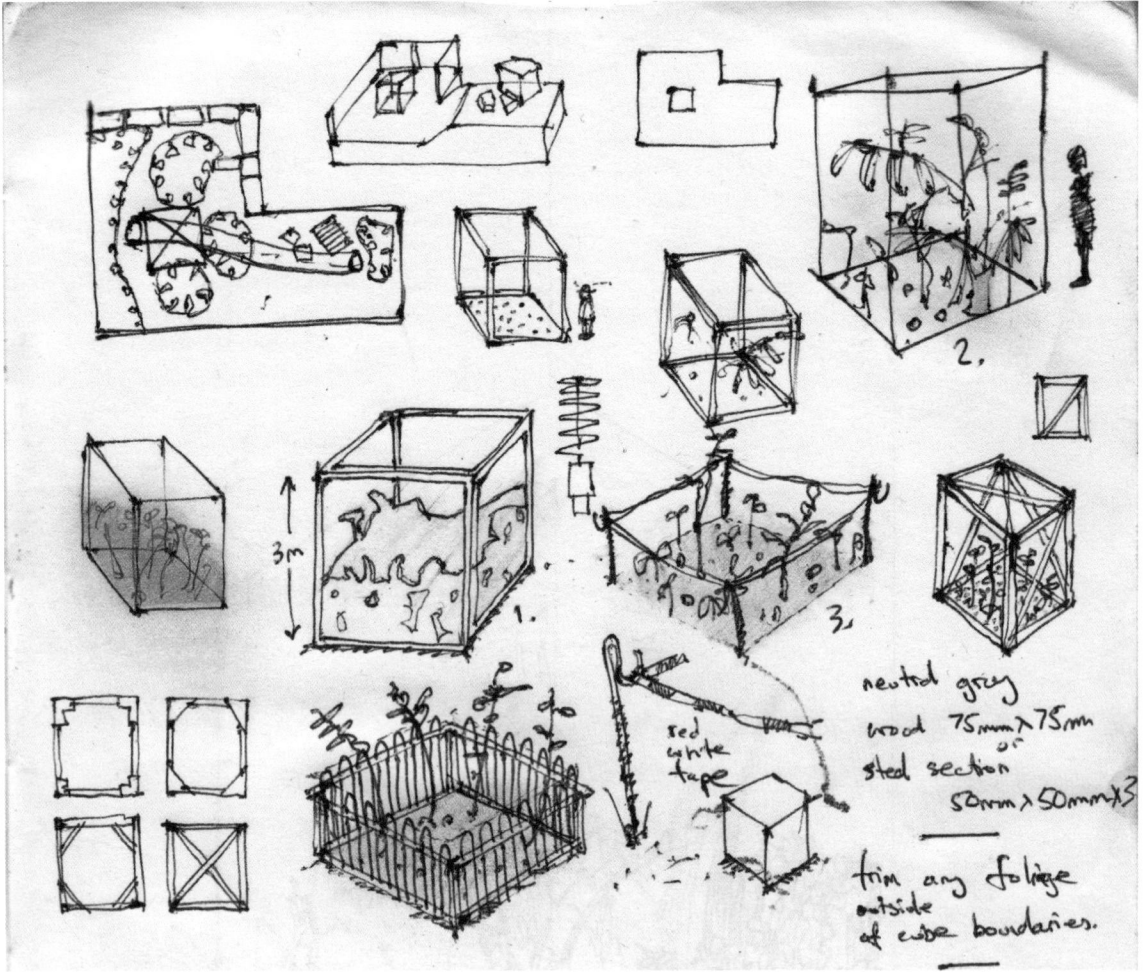

3m

1.

2.

3.

neutral grey
wood 75mm x 75mm
or
steel section
50mm x 50mm x 3

trim any foliage
outside
of cube boundaries.

red
white
tape

18

NOTE ON ART BOOK PUBLISHING

Matthew Cheeseman

I was asked to write 'a note on the reality of art publishing' by the book's editors and a few words on these drawings. It struck me that they are the same piece. We couldn't get this book published by a traditional publisher. There isn't the market. AND Publishing agreed to stock a digital, print on demand edition, whilst we would produce a print version privately. The 'reality of art publishing' is pretty similar to the 'reality' of academic publishing. There are too many producers. Many of the readers are students, people you work with or advertise to personally. Readerships are coerced from personal connections.

There is a sense within academia that this state of affairs amounts to a form of systemic overproduction. The funding system and job market instil a 'publish or die!' attitude: it almost doesn't matter what you publish, just that you do, as much as possible. This brings up questions of value: what is more important, the surface or the substance? I am sure there are parallels to art publishing and beyond. We are all producers now.

The drawings are excerpts from the sketchbooks of Tim Lewis, the third artist on the project. He had to drop out because he had a son and couldn't commit anymore. A similar situation to Dr. Tom Stafford, a psychologist on the project who had a daughter and also had to drop out. Tom actually wrote a piece inspired by Tim's work which would be better placed to accompany these drawings, but it was published by the BBC and we don't have the rights to reproduce it. You can look it up online, but only if you're outside the UK as it was published by BBC Worldwide, who aren't supported by the licensing fee.

Anyway, these sketches are ideas Tim had for the project. This page details a wireframe box or fence which was intended to demarcate an area of Furnace Park. Nothing would be done to the land inside, which would be left to grow unkempt and unaided. Tim thought that this would act as a control, a kind of rolling memory of the project. It wasn't built. This book is now the only record of the wasteland that was, before the land was cleared and made safe, levelled and wood-chipped. I don't think we've included any photos of Furnace Park as it looks now. Our project happened before it came to be, when there was more wildness to it, if wildness is something you can have more or less of. The tethered faun on the next page is an inhabitant of this place. Explorer, native, captive and guard.

While these sketches may evoke a sense of compulsion, of working out an idea for its own sake, I did pressurise Tim to produce them. I did pay him for them. This makes me think how complex and long life can seem to be: I first met Tim at the beginning of the millennium, when I worked for the art gallery that represents him. I helped install one of his shows. Along one wall we exhibited pages from his notebooks, just like these. I remember a couple came into the gallery while we were getting ready and took one of the pages, thinking they were free. It shouldn't have happened and it was my fault for not watching them.

I was excited about working with Tim again and never questioned that I'd have to work for free to do so. That's just something I am used to, as an 'academic' willingly working a collection of limited contracts that don't pay the breadth of my ambition. So these words were written for free. I suppose I am getting kudos in return. No doubt we'll give most of the copies of this book away too: the University of Sheffield via the Crucible programme is paying for them and deserves many thanks for that. So I suppose this is my point about the 'reality of art/academic publishing': the so-called bottom-line values of the market are all buried, covered up and crossed out in a hidden sketchbook of other values, desires and motivations. Tim and Tom left this project because of their family commitments, everyone else donated their spare time, working for free. The 'reality' of working in art and working in universities is something that cannot be subsumed by the market principle because they also operate in a gift economy. Much of the anger and frustration that comes from the monetisation of everything is that it cloaks this gift economy in shame. Giving away one's labour for free is not the problem because work, art, writing should/can be self-realizing. This sense of shame is the one thing I've come to terms with during this project.

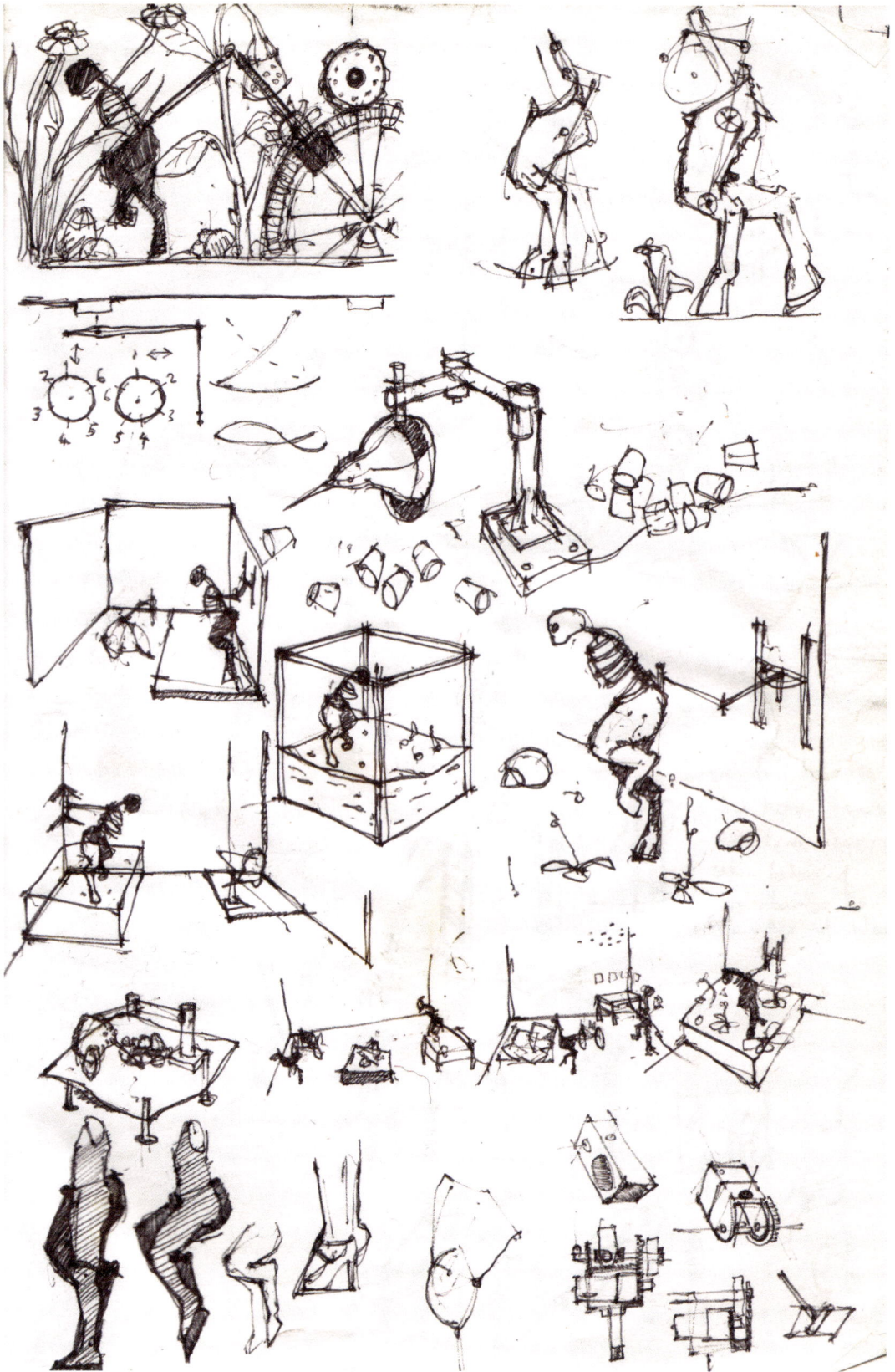

SO, WHAT IS THIS ALL ABOUT?

Arne Schröder

A reflection on collaboration between scientists and artists.

When thinking about what to write in my contribution to this volume, I once again read the original grant proposal whose success primed the pump for our researcher-artist collaboration project. According to the proposal, the aim was 'to develop innovative and experimental collaborations between researchers and artists to transform cities and address urban problems'. What immediately struck me was the apparent contrast between this rather grandiose objective and what we actually did. Even when considering the usual over-ambitiousness and pretentiousness of such funding proposals, it feels like our claims and the project's reality do not match. Did we really transform Sheffield? What urban problems did we look at? Was it not just a lot of inconsequential meetings and vague talking? No, definitely not! While the lack of a solid, physical outcome like a novel research finding or a piece of art was maybe frustrating at times, it actually was the deliberately experimental and open character of the project right from the start that made the whole experience so worthwhile.

When in February 2013 we met for the first time at the Furnace Park site, followed by lunch in the pub, I believe most of us, or at least me, imagined that at the end we would have done what scientists and artists normally do: publish research papers or produce objects of art, only this time with some form of contribution by the other camp. How this contribution was supposed to have made the research or art more novel or different from the usual stuff, I had no idea. I was even quite sceptical and in fact it didn't really happen. But while these things would have been a solid outcome and visible demonstration of the project's success, at the end we achieved something much more valuable and lasting.

Triggered off by the online blogging project we started visiting each other's studios, offices and laboratories, met again at Furnace Park or symposia or hung out together in coffee shops and pubs. All this actually only really took off after the blog had come to its official end. And it was during these personal face-to-face meetings with all their so seemingly vague, inconsequential talking that we were exposed to novel ideas and concepts which opened our minds to collaborating with each other. We established relationships with each other and we even developed new friendships. And it is these things that ultimately provide the fertile ground on which often the most interesting research ideas and creative projects grow and which will finally, in later years, contribute to our so grandiose project aim. And in fact, this is what is happening right now based on close collaborations between several of us.

So what I learned regarding interdisciplinary projects is that you need to take your time, develop a personal relationship, sit back and let ideas grow and mature, instead of rushing and doing something just for the sake of doing it. Given the divide in how scientists and artists explore the world and the formats they use to express their findings, this holds even more for collaborations between them. We would not have been exposed to other ways of thinking and exploring had our project been precisely outlined and timelimited, with a well defined outcome. In contrast, NO PICNIC gave us the time and freedom to set the foundations for great things to come. The blogging was a necessary and helpful start, but it could not replace more personal meetings. I guess this is true for any human endeavour: we are social beings and direct talking to each other is what we do.

GROUND INVESTIGATIONS, A REFLECTION

Bob Levene

It started as an invitation to have a conversation, a one month online exchange of ideas and thoughts. When looking back it was the very notion of dialogue that became not only the means and the process by which this project happened but also the subject and the artwork. With dialogue comes the act of listening, listening without any other intent. With listening comes a building of relationships and understanding and with that can come a new found respect. With respect came support and from that came a genuine space for experimentation and play. From my perspective this was the strength of the project.

The Ground Investigations was our first real world play day and it came from the desire to be working together in the same space with an awareness of each others' practices but without any forced collaboration, need to resolve our thinking or make art. It was simply a fixed space and time for play.

Play is an incredibly serious affair, play is where we learn, discover and uncover without knowing too much about what we are looking for. Play is what artists do. Novel solar cameras were built, surfaces were scanned, passers-by were stopped in the streets, questions were asked, we looked up, down and directly ahead. We talked, walked, made contact with the ground and explored different ways of recording, observing, gathering, documenting, measuring and being in a space in order to understand what that space was. It was a very supportive and equally inspiring environment to work in, seeing everyone doing their own thing gave people permission to carry on or to ask for a hand or an opinion from time to time.

When Hester and myself were given the task to devise or propose a final outcome for the project we both very quickly rejected the idea of producing an installed artwork or object of some kind, it didn't seem to have any relevance to the project. We were keen to continue with the same process and values—dialogue, open-ended conversation, sharing, durational or time based events and without relying on or unpicking the preconceived roles and divisions between artists and researchers. There the concept of the Breakfast was born, the toast became the opportunity for everyone to have their own voice in and about the project.

For myself this dialogue is continuing beyond the project, as a result of meeting the engineering based researchers I am now the Faculty of Engineering's artist-in-residence. The dialogue and listening has become a core part of the process, and I have spent time meeting with engineers finding out about what they do and trying to unpick what it means to engineer something. I've asked them and recorded their hopes, wishes and fears, all of which is feeding into a larger series of works exploring the ground (under), surface, infrastructure and resources.

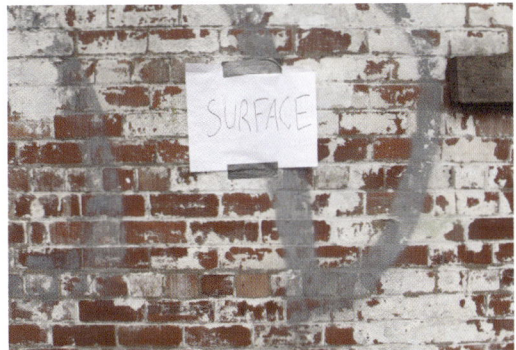

AFTER A FASHION

Alison Beck

Several visits to Furnace Park saw it change from being bare, brown and grey in February to much greener and leafier in May and July.

As the park seemed to be constantly changing, I wanted to record a sense of the place and the people via microscopic details. On the 1st July 2013, I used a microscope to collect images relating to the people who were there. I documented their shoes, clothes, jewellery and tattoos to show Furnace Park after a fashion. The greenery that had grown up had hidden a lot of discarded or lost objects and rubbish. I took images of some interesting items that I found, to convey the wasteland.

Since those images were taken, Furnace Park has been stripped back to the bare concrete, the rubbish cleared, holes filled in and collapsing masonry secured. Now the site is safe, larger numbers of people can visit as the next phase of change begins.

The micrographs are shown with some comments from the wearer of the item being imaged. Partial snapshots of the etymology of the word describing the items are shown on the pictures to illustrate some of the history of these words and where they may have originated from. Like Furnace Park, their form and meaning has changed over time and continues to develop.

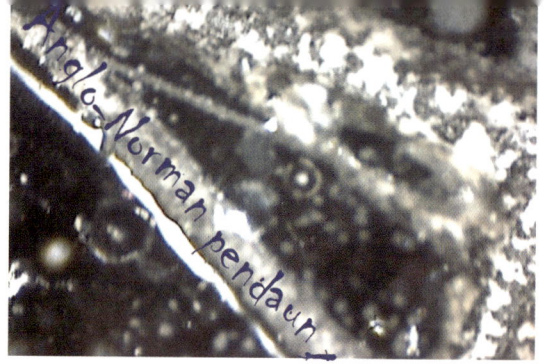

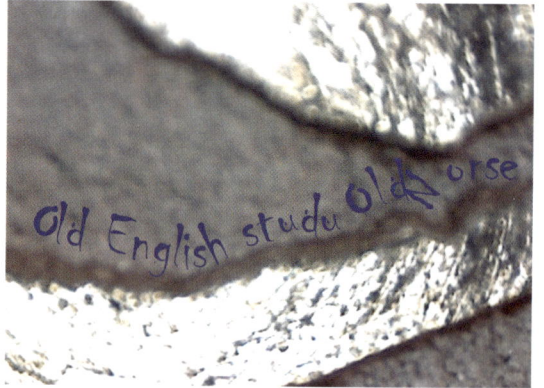

These images suit my tastes: dark, metallic, shiny and textural, almost oily. They look beautiful in the abstract yet strangely similar!

For a ring which looks relatively shiny to the naked eye, the deep scratches and pitting shows a completely different surface to that which I am used to seeing every day.

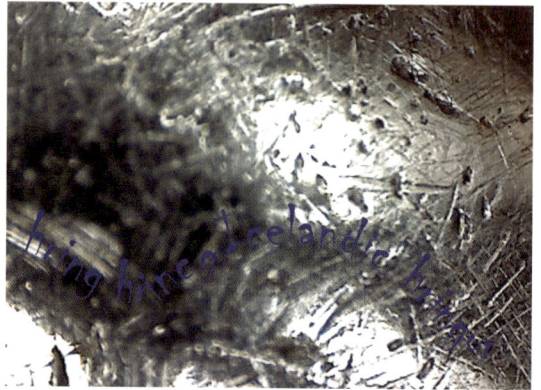

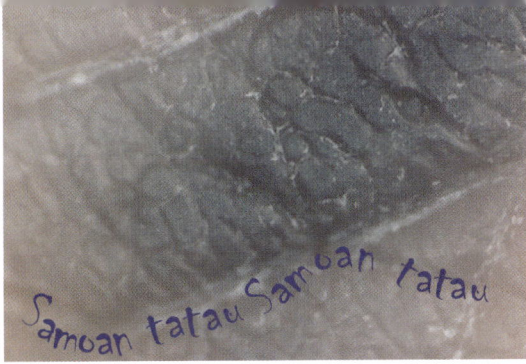

Samoan tatau Samoan tatau

middle English shoo Old Engliz

I wonder how small you can weave?

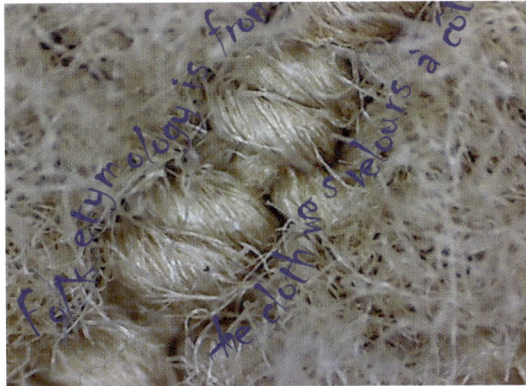

felt etymology is from ... the clothing she/ours ...

Old French bracelet bracchiale

I think I prefer how this bracelet looks close up.

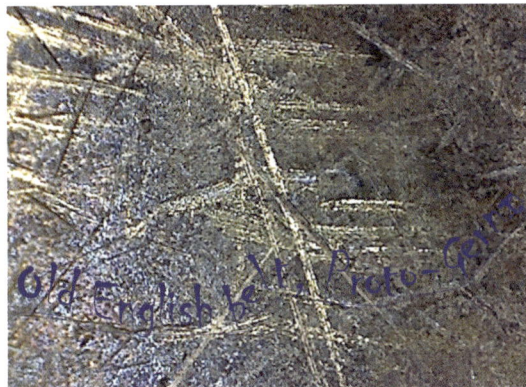

Old English belt Proto-Germ...

I've already thrown one of these away, it's either been incinerated or lives in landfill. The other two I keep close. One will last for a long time, longer than me, while the other will go when I die.

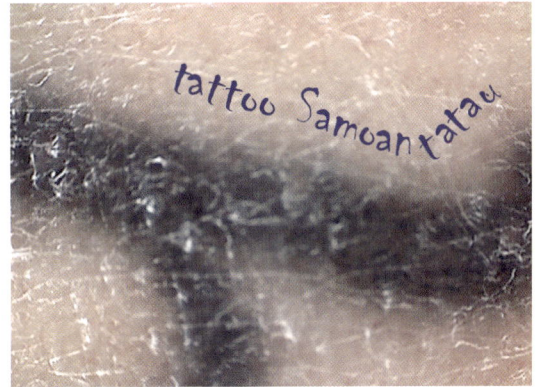

tattoo Samoan tatau

Fascinating image of the stitching on my shoe, clearly showing that the stitching is composed of synthetic fibres.

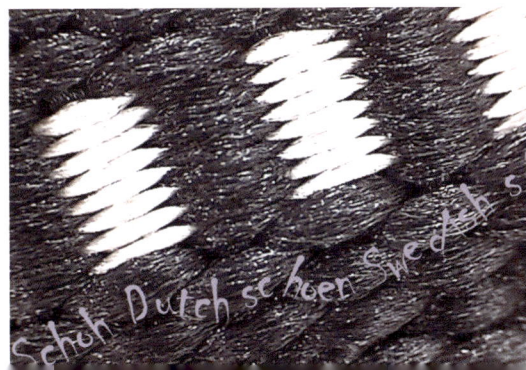

Schoh Dutch schoen Swedish sk...

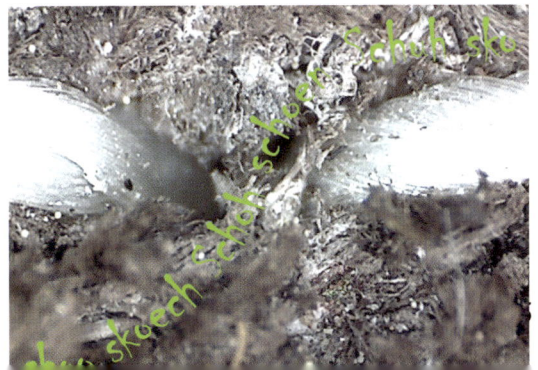

...hu skoech schoe schoen schoh sko

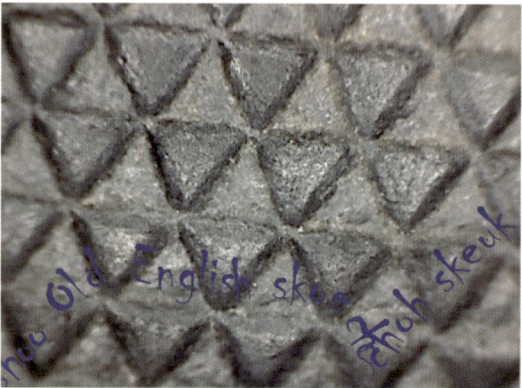

I've walked for miles in this shoe.

This t-shirt looks more like a woolly jumper.

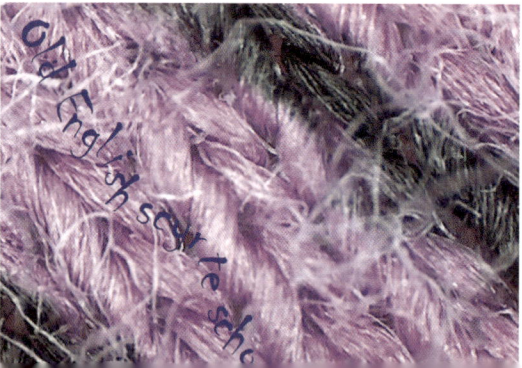

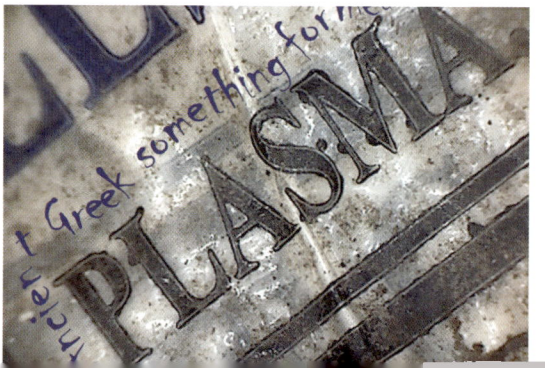

Plasma is a state of matter consisting of partially ionized gas. I use cool plasmas to prepare coatings to control the surface chemistry of materials such as plastics, glass, metals.

GOLD FINCHES

Sarah Spencer

Goldfinches are nearly five times more likely to be seen in British gardens than they were during the mid-1990s.

Around 313,000 pairs breed in the UK each year. In winter, many goldfinches migrate as far south as Spain. They are commonly kept and bred in captivity around the world because of their distinctive appearance and lovely liquid twittering song. Because of the thistle seeds it eats (and teasel seeds, as seen in Furnace Park) in Christian symbolism the goldfinch is associated with Christ's crown of thorns. In pictures of Madonna and Child the goldfinch sometimes appears to represent the foreknowledge of the crucifixion (see Raphael's Madonna of the Goldfinch). They also feature as a natural luxury in Keats' 1884 poem 'I stood tip-toe upon a little hill'.

My drawing of the goldfinch represents some themes from the interviews I held with researchers:

1. the widening appreciation of art beyond the image
2. personal entitlement to the creative process
3. a mindfulness in observing our surroundings
4. that distinctions between artist and researcher were explored in relation to producing, understanding, generating.

ANALYSING THE SURFACE OF FURNACE PARK FROM ABOVE

Jonathan Paragreen

During the Ground Investigations, whilst most other participants were getting very close up to the surface, I tried to view the surface from farther away.

I achieved this by attaching an old camera phone to a long stick found on the site, the camera was set to take a shot every 10 seconds allowing time to move into a new location and set up the shot. Further improvements were made for use at future events which allow for control of the camera by any Wi-Fi enabled mobile device and for the user to view the live video stream or to take high quality still images.

1. Live video stream from camera broadcast over Wi-Fi.
2. Motorola Defy phone installed with free IP Webcam app.
3. Control of camera and ability to view live images in the browser of any Wi-Fi enabled device.
4. Wi-Fi router powered by 12V battery.

The images looking down on walls and fences give a great sense of perspective and from angles at which we are not used to viewing such structures.

These are some images taken by using the pole to move the camera around a hole in the concrete. These images give a fantastic view of the different materials used in the construction of the surface upon which the site stands, showing the brick, concrete and the rusting steel reinforcements.

The images which I find the least interesting are those of the surface of the park. These images lack a sense of scale and contrast which is gained with the close-up images of the vegetation.

People, in my opinion, make some of the most interesting photographic compositions. I love the squinting, looking-up-to-the-camera poses.

CHANGE

Jonathan Paragreen

'So you are making people unemployed' was my grandfather's response when I told him I was working on an engineering education scheme to automate a process at a local business.

Old copper mine at Parys Mountain, Anglesey

Steel works at Redcar, Teesside

Engineering is all about making changes, whether that is the design of a new structure, infrastructure, a new process, machinery or a new product. As an engineer I have always loved the challenge of solving a technical problem above all else. In contrast, conversations about my work (especially with non-engineer family or friends) often focus on the negative impact of engineering. Perhaps I just know a lot of negative people, but it has struck me that any change will have some negative impact on someone, even though the overall impact of the change may be positive.

Working on NO PICNIC has caused me to reflect on the social impact of engineering and change. The blogging process has had a particularly large impact. Throughout our meetings this theme of creation and destruction has repeatedly been brought up. Our initial conversations were around changing something physical to create something new. Creating a new steel structure requires either the recycling of the steel from existing products or the destruction of an environment for ores. Our later conversations began to consider social implications. We considered that the change of land use for Furnace Park would have significant impact on the sex workers operating nearby, possibly moving them, which will then also have an impact on wherever they move to. The clearing of the site also caused disappointment to the participants, the vegetation and litter was a large part of our work together. Its loss changed the character of the site, as well as our own feelings of belonging there and our future plans.

> —There's never been good times sin' spinning-
> jennies came up.
> —Machine is th' ruin of poor folk.
> from Mary Barton by Elizabeth Gaskell

Often change is characterised by its negative aspects. Each new technology brings about a period of adjustment. Though change can be tough for the individuals directly involved, fears of mass unemployment due to mechanisation, automation and introduction of robotics have largely been unfounded. People have, however, had to adapt and seek out new opportunities or new careers. Attitudes change over time too and areas where the environment has been

scarred by industry are later appreciated for their beauty and scale, from Victorian mills, modern chemical and steel works through to mines and quarries.

Within engineering, technology tends to come first and social impact has tended to be an afterthought, assessed as an add-on process. Environmental and safety risk assessments and public consultations are carried out after considerable design work. This has steadily improved over recent time with concepts of safety and environmental impact being considered much earlier in the design process, although often this is cost driven to negate the need for costly modifications later on. Many large companies now consider robotics and automation as tools for the workers rather than as a replacement for employees, taking into account the need to retain skills.

The term 'creative destruction' has been applied in many topics, from economics to town planning. It was coined by Joseph Schumpter in the 1950s, to describe how new economic orders arise out of the destruction of previous models. Marx describes the creative-destructive cycle of capitalist forces as leading to their eventual downfall. The term was also applied by Robert Bruce to his regeneration plans for postwar Glasgow which would have required the mass demolition and rebuilding of a large part of the city centre. It is also a recurring theme in Eastern mysticism with the Hindu god Shiva being both a creator and destroyer.

Perhaps such change is inevitable for some. From those whose house stands in the way of a new railway, motorway, or power line to those employed by an industry being superseded by new technology or policy. Engineers do need to develop a greater awareness of the social impact of new technology on individuals and consider how to best minimise this, but change will continue to happen and individuals will have to continue to adapt as long as populations continue to grow and our consumption continues to rise and change. And even for those negatively impacted this can provide a chance to relocate, a change or a push to start something else. It is not all bad, but sometimes it is good for all of us to reflect on what is being destroyed.

TAXONOMISING RESEARCH

Sarah Spencer

We sit within macro demographic categories based on age, socioeconomic status, gender, nationality, ethnicity, sexuality. Although these categories appear straightforward they are difficult to both conceptualise and measure. Socioeconomic status, for example, can include data such as wealth, occupation, the occupation of parents, housing status, education level.

There are also local categories that we find ourselves within, ones which we create through interactions centred on a common set of beliefs, behaviours, purposes and interests. Academics have studied groups based around these communities of practice. An example would be the work of Penelope Eckert, a sociolinguistic who studied jocks (school-oriented) versus burnouts (locally-oriented) in a Detroit high school in the 80s. Such communities might form anywhere—in staffrooms, online, at the school gates, in youth clubs and nightclubs.

And then there are the consumer-based categories according to which we are constantly categorised. These locate us according to our vital statistics, which might include demographic data but also information accumulated from our daily behaviour, both online and offline. An example of such a classification system is 'A Classification of Residential Neighbourhoods' (Acorn). Acorn provides data on the consumption and lifestyle patterns of people living in a particular postcode. According to their website 'Acorn segments postcodes and neighbourhoods into 6 Categories, 18 Groups and 62 Types. By analysing significant social factors and population behaviour, it provides precise information and in-depth understanding of the different types of people'. This expression, 'types of people', is a recurring turn of phrase in their reports. Postcode searches produce categories of 'types' and descriptions of their behaviour that appear to legitimise assumptions about what people have access to and how people behave. The following examples are direct extracts from the longer profiles provided by Acorn for areas that matter to me.

My childhood home

Fewer than usual of these people access the internet. Those who do, use the web relatively infrequently, possibly for gambling or playing games. Offline some will enjoy going to play bingo. Others will gamble and play the lottery.

My recent address

A higher than usual proportion might be active switchers of their financial accounts and have recently obtained new credit cards. Some people are only repaying the minimum each month and some will be using their overdraft. Similarly more than usual will have modest savings and ISAs.

The streets around Furnace Park

You have searched on a postcode where the bulk of the residents are not living in private households. This covers various circumstances.

1. People may be in communal establishments yet still consumers to some degree, for example living on military bases or on holiday in hotels.
2. They may be unlikely to be active consumers, for example residents of care homes or medical establishments.
3. The postcode might represent a business or industrial park with no residents.

When searches of local postcodes do come back with detailed profiles, they vary widely from one street to the next. One street very near to Furnace Park reads:

This type comprises halls of residence, purpose-built private sector student accommodation and streets with high proportions of privately rented student flats. Ownership of smartphones, iPhones, Blackberry and Android phones, will be well above average, as will the proportion owning tablet and hand-held computers. Their interests may focus around sports, films and going out. Some may regularly go to the gym to attend exercise, dance or similar classes. Film, computing, educational and style magazines may be their preferred reading matter. The kind of high street names this type might favour includes New Look, Topshop, Topman, River Island, H&M, or La Senza. Coffee shops, pizza and burger shops are also likely to find favour.

A street or two away from this and the profile changes to:

Single elderly people and young single parents are both found more frequently than average in these flats. Most of the flats are rented from the council or social housing provider, although a few will be owned. The properties in this type will tend to be mid-rise and high-rise buildings often in cities and larger towns. The numbers claiming Jobseeker's

Allowance might be three times the national average. Similarly high proportions might be claiming benefits relating to single parents, or to disabilities. Over a third of households may be living entirely on some form of benefits In general relatively few people will have many educational qualifications. Those working are likely to be in routine jobs. These will be poorly paid. These areas include some of the greatest concentrations of people with lowest incomes. Under half of the people in these areas earn sufficient to pay tax. They will shop in cheaper high street stores such as Iceland and buy hot food from the likes of Greggs or McDonald's.

These multi-layered processes of categorisation are being constantly applied by retailers, researchers, politicians and, of course, by all of us in our mundane and everyday judgements of each other. I'm Northern. I am an infrequent member of a life-drawing class. I shop weekly in Morrisons and eat McNuggets. What are you?

Furnace Park and forgetting

I signed up to the collaboration because I saw Furnace Park as a very unusual opportunity to work with a diverse range of people who lived and worked nearby. I was interested in the challenge of a public engagement project which aimed to meaningfully engage with people who live near each other but who have very different lifestyles. Looking back, I can see how much of this enthusiasm rested on demographic assumptions and an implicit subscription to Acorn's principles of market categorisation.

In the end, our project did not bring together members of different local communities in a shared practice. Instead, we—researchers and artists—became a new community of practice. One which met to reflect on a site of forgotten industrial land tucked down the road from the University. In this newly formed taxonomic group, we practiced forgetting what we'd learned to be. Our professional identity was the reason why we were in the park, and yet it was temporarily stripped back to a set of disconnected perspectives once we were there.

In this project, I was not really an academic speech therapist with all that might involve.* Unexpectedly, my habit of drawing small bits of the world felt relevant at the periphery as, in the park, we watched ants disturbed under a stone, wondered about a pile of whitening empty snail shells, and watched unexpected goldfinches balance in thistles. My hatred of the social apartheid to be witnessed in shops such as Waitrose** shifted in focus as I reflected on who would have access to this ex-industrial site and why. My interest in forgotten urban spaces became important as the project became an opportunity to examine beauty in a form that is not usually recognised. When I was a graduate speech and language therapist, I worked in Redcar on the coast just south of the River Tees. The steel manufactured in Redcar makes up the Tyne Bridge in my hometown, and for that matter, the Sidney Harbour Bridge is made of it too. I love the steelworks which sprawled along the end of the estuary. I loved passing the fire and smoke these works emitted on the train. I enjoyed the contrast between the beauty of the local beach and the sheer scale of the site on the horizon. I spent my first wedding anniversary happily marching in coastal mud behind a fish market and docks on a walk between Cleethorpes and Grimsby. Now here I was with a group of people reflecting on the beauty and changing value of a disused area of concrete and weeds.

We put down our professional identities. By doing this, the paradoxical outcome was that we had space to reconnect new or seemingly irrelevant forms of being. The experience served to trouble what we were and to reconsider who we considered ourselves to be. The project allowed different parts of me—perhaps us—to achieve legitimacy and relevance within the processes of knowing and understanding.

Categorising equality

This project changed perceptions of who we are and how we understand the process of understanding. This will have long-term consequences for our work. As an academic and clinician, I've always worked within working class communities affected by deindustrialisation. My research is concerned with securing equal outcomes for children and young people from different socioeconomic backgrounds. I'm currently writing up data about a group of young people I worked with in a socially disadvantaged community who were far less likely to do well in their GCSEs when compared to peers in a more affluent area (24% achieved five or more A* to C grades at GCSE compared to 61%). I discuss this in relation to their language abilities (such as their use and understanding of complex words and sentences). I investigate how language and educational engagement and attainment relate to wider social inequalities.

As reported by the Sheffield Fairness Commission, an hour's bus journey on the Number 83 through the city shows how stark these inequalities are. The journey starts at Millhouses, where a woman can expect to live around 86.3 years. By the time the number 83 comes down Ecclesall Road and into the city, a woman can expect to live 81.6 years and by the time it journeys up into Burngreave (40 minutes after you've got on the bus); a woman can expect to live just 76.9 years. Despite social injustice across the UK, public attitudes towards inequality are unsympathetic. The move away from a rhetoric of social class towards that of social exclusion within political discussion and research alike has promoted the idea that an individual's lack of aspirations and poor response to opportunity leads to their social exclusion. The emergence of 'chav', along with scroungers and spongers, to describe a section of the working class has been described by Diane Reay as 'an almost Victorian middle class horror at the indignities of poverty'. Despite the known scandal of tax evasion and the estimated £16bn worth of benefits unclaimed by working and unemployed people, we buy into the myth that the £1.2bn benefit fraud bill is a key factor in the UK economy's crisis.

My research has the potential to have a wider social impact outside of academia: collaborating with teachers, increasing children's language skills, supporting children to do well in school, increasing educational attainment, reducing educational inequality. Obviously, I think this work is very important and put faith in the value of the research projects I am involved with.

A persistent issue worries me though. In order to address social injustice, you need to define those affected by it. This means that as a researcher, I subscribe to some form of demographic categorisation. Some form of identification criteria is needed whether we want to support children who are working class, socially excluded, hard to reach, disadvantaged or underachieving. Quantifying or describing people's background and the identities attached to them is complex and it risks simplifying people's lives and even pathologising them. In my research field, participants are discussed in terms of their parents' educational background, occupation and income. Participants' language skills and educational attainment are problematized. By demonstrating unsupported difficulties and underachievement, research can be used to build a case for further funding, further academic intervention, further professional support. This financial reality, one that underpins and informs most research these days, resonates with Acorn's reductive interests, where social categorisation has been drawn up for financial and instrumental gain. This process of measuring relative socioeconomic status, language, education, and so on, reminds me of Acorn's attempt to reduce people to a measure of their capitalist potential. It also risks accidentally confirming the societal prejudices that are held about working class communities in the UK. In other words, children from socially disadvantaged homes do less well in school because of a combination of their parents' background and their language skills. Because of my own background, this operation feels like a betrayal.

At first, this current project appeared relevant to my research as it offered a chance to bring together communities with different economic backgrounds and overcome local prejudices. Our work didn't do that (perhaps the park will pick up this aim later), but the project did help to reassert my unease at the role of categorising identity in my own practice. The project was a catalyst for me to abandon some of the endless tensions involved in research and clinical practice within socioeconomically disadvantaged communities. Essentially, the project did this by allowing me space to shed my own professional identity within a work capacity and to learn without defending my own expertise. The project did not bring different members of the local community into Furnace Park in the name of public engagement, as I once hoped it would. Instead, it reaffirmed the potential of dialogue between people with different perspectives as a means of developing new shared understanding. This project gestured towards a potential solution to the challenges faced within my research discipline. I now look forward to engaging in meaningful dialogue with research 'participants' as a way of co-investigating the complexity of social justice, language and education (research taxonomies suspended).

*As with any identity, it takes sustained effort to construct the identity of an academic speech therapist. Endless small acts create this identity: the activity of reviewing articles, updates to my website, books read, contributions to meetings, maintaining my Health and Care Professions Council registration and Royal College of Speech and Language Therapists membership, the completion of professional logs, my conformity to information governance, my work with service users. Outfits, books, presentations, stationary. My role could be defined by what it seeks to measure: trainee therapist attainment, children's language skills, scholastic success, the impact of a paper, the significance of a finding, the performance on a standardised vocabulary assessment in relation to published norms, the evidence base of interventions, student satisfaction, an applicant's potential, interviewees performance in relation to The 6 Cs (Care, Compassion, Competence, Communication, Courage, Commitment), schools' engagement with research. I know, for example, that the word 'measure' has the phoneme ʒ in the middle of it, a 'sh' with voice added, a post-alveolar fricative (also found in 'dysphagia' and 'pleasure'). In the project, standing in Furnace Park, there was a lot to forget in order to become immersed in the process of new understandings, a lot to forget without capitalising on all that has gone before.

**As The Independent and other media reported on 30th December 2013 Waitrose faced revolt from the regular middle-class customer who was concerned that a free coffee deal was attracting the wrong type of clientele.

FOOTPRINTS: MAPPING THE LEGACY OF THE FURNACE

Caroline Evans

Furnace Park lies within easy walking distance of the city centre, not more than 25 minutes at a reasonable pace, but it feels distinct—in places, almost isolated—and relatively quiet, despite proximity to the Inner Ring Road and the hum of traffic this provides.

The furnace in Furnace Park refers to a cementation furnace, built in 1848 for crucible steel production. Ever since the start of the project, I was intrigued by the red bricked conical shaped structure which I'd been told was of historical significance in terms of metallurgy in Sheffield. It stands intact, alone, fenced off, surrounded on three sides by the car park of the HSBC Bank, across the road from the Furnace Park site and diagonally opposite to the Don Cutlery Works. It is a Scheduled Ancient Monument, Grade II listed by English Heritage [Building ID: 457046], described as 'the sole survivor of a characteristic industrial building once numerous in Sheffield'. A striking fact and remarkable, particularly considering that, by 1860 there were reportedly 250 cementation furnaces across the city.

The nearby Don Cutlery Works is also Grade II listed by English Heritage [Building ID: 501152], described as a 'Purpose-built cutlery works. Red brick, part-rendered, some stone dressings, slate roofs with brick gable and eaves stacks. A purpose-built, mid-to-late C19 integrated works, with a typical layout of large front range, probably housing offices, warehouses, and workshops, a yard reached through a covered cart entrance, around which are arranged a number of workshop ranges, at least one of which has individual hand forges on the ground floor. This type of complex is very distinctive to the industrial identity of Sheffield'.

The red bricks of both structures are readily visible from the Furnace Park site. Both feature in many photos taken there. Together the furnace and Don Cutlery Works reflect steel making and the metal working trades (tools, cutlery, saws etc.) that are key to the industrial heritage of Sheffield. I set out to investigate their legacy by looking for footprints, asking what remains of these activities in the area: are there remnants, echoes, reminders of the heritage of the industrial revolution that occurred here? I was inspired to do this by the skyline views from the park, which showed a mix of old and new buildings, wondering what lay beyond and how it had a relationship to the site. I set out on foot, with a camera, to explore and record buildings, place names and their usage. This area was new to me, despite working relatively close by.

What did I find? From thinking there'd be only a few key locations to photograph, I quickly realised that there is something of potential interest round every corner. Repeated trips would undoubtedly reveal more. It seemed essential that I let my first impressions guide me. It was therefore necessary to accept that I couldn't catalogue to completion, but instead make lists of what I did find, then work from there. Photographs were taken en route from Newcastle Street (Furnace Hill Conservation Area) and the area beyond Furnace Park, mainly Kelham Island, another designated Conservation Area which lies northwest of the city centre. These areas feel quite distinct as the Inner Ring Road effectively cuts through and circumscribes the area to some degree. The Kelham Island area is crossed by the River Don, around which industry grew up as water was used to drive water wheels to power the workshops.

My first impressions of the new purpose-built flats and derelict buildings (including former industrial sites, with 'works' in their names) changed when I quickly realised that businesses centred on steel are still in production (metal products, saws, scissors). This isn't simply an industrial wasteland re-colonised for residential purposes.

The legacy of the furnace is everywhere, not only as industrial heritage, which is formally archived and displayed at Kelham Island Museum, where a Bessemer converter for mass production of steel dominates the external display, but also in the characteristics of the locality. People not only once worked, but are working here, they also live here, play here. The infrastructure and place names reflect that. New housing developments on sites of former works are both new builds (e.g. Cornwall Works) and renovations of listed buildings or factory sites (e.g. Brooklyn Works, Cornish Place). This mix of use reflects 'pull down and build new' and 'conservation based' approaches. The Little Kelham development is converting the former Green Lane Works site and Eagle Works into sustainable zero carbon eco-friendly project housing, retaining and restoring the landmark Green Lane clock tower entrance. Cafés (Grind Café, The Works Café), and leisure activities (Foundry Climbing Centre) indicate that Kelham Island is thriving despite the presence of many buildings with broken windows and a derelict feel to some streets, amongst which I got a bit lost and disorientated whilst absorbed in taking photographs. Business names are still clearly legible from some derelict signs (Wilson and Murray Surface and Grinding, Williams Brothers Sheffield). I also saw graffiti. For example, at the Don Cutlery Works I saw boarded up, street-facing windows being painted blue by a workman on one of my visits, and then painted over with art work at a later date.

This project certainly taught me to 'see differently'. First impressions of the area around Furnace Park and my explorations of the building infrastructure were both very surface, in the sense that I simply photographed what took my attention as having a connection to the theme of footprints. I think these images represent my shifting perspective on the space, and also provide a route to cohesive reflection on the links to space which I chose to explore empirically, with minimum prior research.

As an end note, on my travels I found a derelict building labelled 'Footprint Tools'. This seemed apt in terms of my plan and reinforced my selection of 'footprints' as the title for this piece. I was pleased to find that although this site is empty, Footprint Tools have simply relocated within Sheffield, to Admiral Works.

Ground Exploration by Bob Levene.
Taken during Sheffield Boundary Walk, a project by Ian Nesbitt and Bob Levene.
Photo by Ian Nesbitt.

THAT WAS ALWAYS THE WORRY

Sarah Spencer

Towards the end of the project, I met with the
artists and researchers to discuss the nature of the
collaboration, the benefits and challenges of the
process and whether the project was likely to result in
any changes to their wider practice. Quotes from these
informal interviews begin the book.

Two themes emerged. The first was enjoyment as a form of lightness and playfulness. Collaborators gave an account of the project as a break from professional routine and discipline. The second theme was the focus on the process of the collaboration rather than any defined outcomes or outputs: 'That was always the worry, "we're enjoying this too much"'.

The three expectations below are based on artist Hannah Hull's discussion of why art produced via social inclusion activities is only accepted by the art world as Outsider Art (http://hannahhull.co.uk/page14.htm).

1. Any personal therapeutic element of the result of art or research practice is rarely discussed.
2. There is a tradition of the artwork or research existing in its own right: the practitioners' biography is not often regarded as essential to the reading of the work.
3. Work is often produced in relation to a user, audience or reader.

Our project went some way towards violating all three of these expectations. Perhaps this is why it felt so very unusual. Collaborators' enjoyment and personal satisfaction within the project was reported with a tinge of guilt, which seems unwarranted given that most of the project was completed outside of our contracted hours, in our 'own time' (as though the time in the lab and office isn't inhabited by us). What is the role of playfulness in research? What happens when our practice has a benefit for the researcher or artist? Doesn't research frequently result in a benefit for the researcher (increased funding, a promotion, increased prestige?). Was the project any more than a form of training? Does it matter if the benefits for the collaborators include some kind of release or therapeutic element?

In the absence of goals or the production of an output to be displayed publically, our focus shifted to the process of knowing and understanding. The project offered a space to think about processes of constructing new meaning: examining the nature of things, experiential knowledge and methods of representation. The project also allowed reflection on the process of collaborative endeavour: meaningful engagement, forming new partnerships and shared perspectives.

Although the shift from outcomes to process sounds abstract, the collaborators were able to give concrete everyday examples of how they would refocus on processes more generally within their daily role. For example: in incorporating a greater openness in designing future research applications, creating increased space within PhD supervision roles for independent experimentation and risk of failure, leaving room for free experimentation and exploration within future research design.

The project's emphasis on processes has led me to focus more in my own work on the physical activity involved in data collection. Sitting on a tram, occupying the physical environment of secondary schools, travelling through council estates. I've also been inspired by Bob's boundary walks to complete my own walks, in areas similar to those where I've conducted research in the past. Some of the resulting photos of Skye Edge, Manor Top and Park Hill in Sheffield are included in this book. I didn't set off on these walks to achieve a goal or collect data, but to get space to explore my own role in relation to generating understanding. The project has also informed a re-evaluation of my own research practice, prioritising investigation that does not rely exclusively on objective measurement. I work weekly at a local youth club (in a community in which I've conducted research into language and socioeconomic disadvantage in the past). I'm volunteering without a goal or research agenda: just to engage and see where the process takes me.

FIELD POEM

Matthew Cheeseman

Bob and Hester set up the Ground Investigations and asked us to spend the day doing what we do, but exploring Furnace Park, working alongside everyone else.

I work by writing, so I thought I would do that. I thought I'd write a poem. After a while trying, I decided that was a bad idea. Then I hit upon photographing all the words scattered in the park: words on crisp packets, scraps of paper and on the side of cans. Even though the whole place appeared pretty clean, when you looked around slowly, methodically, you couldn't help but find rubbish and litter. There were words everywhere. Because the park is at the edge of a red light district there were plenty of condom wrappers, at least 40, probably more. It struck me, at the time, how unlikely it was that previous owners had ever read the packaging beyond the brand name. This thought quickly turned to the words I produced for universities.

As I foraged around in the waste, I thought about writing this piece. I wanted to use all the words I'd photographed, transcribe them perhaps, blow up the photos and copy out all the safety warnings and promotional slogans. When it came to doing this though, I couldn't be bothered and no longer saw the point. I reproduce instead the occasional notes I made as I rooted around the site. I suppose you could call it a field text, which would place it within a research methodology I've used a lot: ethnography. But then again, you don't have to call it that. Neither do I. A field poem:

The sound of words—left (let) out—this is not poetry but dirty words.

Very positive impressions when I entered the park— the wildlife, the flowers, light rain. But cataloguing the filth, the condoms and then getting bored of the compulsion: the endless, hidden rubbish... makes the place quite, quite horrid.

Words running through my head. This stops? Pen top off... pushing me into creative writing here— what are the words worth? Anything? And value, again, comes up–into engagement.

An engagement worth of words.

An engagement of words.

Lost brick, where is it? Broken brick with word written on it.

Looking for words thinking how fragile the thinking thoughts are—how easily disrupted and lost and overshadowed by the future text, spreading over the real words from the future, here on the ground.

The brain as both thought (over)production unit and filter system, removing sensory data, focusing in on rubbish, searching, ignoring everything green and

brown, filtering out anything growing or dying, seeking cellophane or chucked aluminium.

Why spend time hunting rubbish? Many other things to do. Everyone busy. It is you doing this, by chance, by route. Does that give you a responsibility? To what, here in this park, uni property?

Is this a collaboration with artists? Who owns these collaborations?

Sarah—Bob conversation. Who owns it?

Sarah—isn't it interesting how we come to the park with ourselves.

Three weeks or so after doing this, I delivered a paper at a symposium entitled 'Critical engagements with engagement'. This was a day I helped plan. Or, at least a day I tried to help fund. Here's an excerpt from my funding application, explaining what the day was about:

The symposium will not frame its discussion of engagement and research impact on specific case studies, but on the critical contexts that surround public engagement. In this way the symposium will be of use to anyone writing research council applications or planning engagement activities. Research areas for consideration include:

Public engagement with higher education; what is at stake when creative practitioners facilitate change in communities; the relationships between the practices of artists and urban policy makers; the line between public engagement as a democratic tool for society's voice and as a mould for society's form; public engagement in industry; public resistance in public engagement; the public's role in academia; the 'participatory turn' and its relational, dialogical and collaborative aesthetics; conceptualising publics; how cultural context inflects public participation; temporality of public engagement; sustainable public engagement; acrimony in public practices.

That was copied from somewhere. I don't understand half of them. The application continues:

This is an apposite time to hold such a symposium. Not only would this be the third public symposium organised around the Furnace Park project, it would also be the first held since the project went live. The park has been granted planning permission and the University has been handed the keys. Work is about to commence on site. A three year arts focused site specific project is about to take place in the University. As a curated site, the park could be an innovative and valuable resource for both the University of Sheffield, the city of Sheffield and even an international community of artists and researchers. Yet at the moment this cultural capital is prospective. The implicit research question of the symposium is, then, how might Furnace Park interface with the engagement of research? This leads on into broader questions of cultural value: what cultural value could and should Furnace Park have, and how can discussions of this potential value inform its development? What will the development of engaging this value displace?

The funding was for £500 to pay for speaker's travel, room hire and food (to encourage people to come along). The application was turned down but the symposium went ahead anyway with funding from another source. If it wasn't for this book those words would never have been read again. Like the rubbish in Furnace Park, my computer is littered with lost words. The paper at this symposium was entitled 'The Threat of Engagement'. Here's the abstract:

This paper will discuss the Sandpit, a project based in Furnace Park. Sandpit is an eight-month long exploratory collaboration between three artists and six researchers. It was explicitly funded by the University of Sheffield Crucible scheme with public engagement in mind. The paper discusses the public's role within the project (and academia), situating them in relation to the two distinct methodologies Sandpit has concerned itself with: scientific method and artistic practice. What was the point of the project? What has been learnt, discovered or encountered? Does it matter and should anyone care beyond the individual participants?

As you may be able to pick up, by this point I was disillusioned and bitter about a whole host of things (all to do with work). I gave quite a confrontational paper. Here are some notes from another file I've found on my computer:

Over the last three years I've been involved in lots of engagement projects at the University of Sheffield... programming films in the cinema, holding a concert for refugees and asylum seekers, putting on an exhibition of Sheffield post-punk music, writing poetry with mathematicians, designing an app that explores Sheffield music culture, using graphic novels with cancer survivors, staging a Throbbing Gristle re-enactment. All have been funded to various degrees, typically AHRC or internal money. One could say I am an engager or an 'engaging researcher'. But I understand the practice very much from the inside, from doing it. I'm not going to formally define engagement because I've never read anything about it, nor been trained in it. I'm not up with the literature. I'm not up with much literature to be honest, even the material in my field. I've been so busy engaging I've forgotten what field I'm in. What research am I engaging? That's never really been a problem, or a question that anyone has asked. As Higher Education has

mutated to accommodate impact and engagement I've had to mutate with it, to respond to the funding out there.

I tried to argue that university funders fetishize an unformed and imaginary 'public', assuming that this 'public' would be interested in the work of researchers if only researchers could learn how to connect with them. It was obvious from the questions I received that I didn't put across my point well and sounded as if I had wilfully ignored my funding remit. It had been a weird morning—I was late for the day because I was stopped by the police for stealing my own bag (true story) and then I had to leave early to meet Bob and Hester to discuss the first iteration of the picnic (which was about to not happen). Luckily I heard Emma Cocker's paper 'Performing the City' before I left. Full of stubborn enthusiasm, I wrote a summary poem:

> rehearsing the mind + body
> in the world, other world, with
> bodies dancing alone
> + together in body +
> mind + place, autonomy
> together
> no self in + from
> forms + space

Despite the poor reception of my own paper I gave a further version at another conference. This time I only have this paragraph, again from a file on my computer:

Unlearning 'being a scientist' unlearning 'being an artist'—what have the artists unlearnt? They are curious... there are different knowledges at play here. A contrast between two different knowledges... the artists with more prestige (in some eyes?), but the scientists with something of more value (in others?), both fancying each other, a bit. And the public was the justification for these knowledges dancing with each other, even if the public never actually got an invite.

The parallels I'm gesturing at here, between words on discarded condom wrappers, words I've sequestered away on my computer and words written in Furnace Park seems a little trite after I've read the contributions of others to this book. I hope the project has made a contribution to people's lives and working practices. Yet there's something about the whole thing that makes me uneasy. I'm still a little angry and embittered. If anything that is what I have gained from this project: an understanding that I am angry and embittered and a realisation of why that might be so.

The first University building I worked in, Sorby Hall was demolished in 2006 by controlled explosion. It was built in 1963, the year the Robbins Report recommended a mass Higher Education system for the UK. Since it fell, the Endcliffe Village was built and following that the buildings of a new, unnamed era: the 24/7 Information Commons, the expanded Union and Jessop West (housing English, History and Modern Languages). The Arts Tower has been remodelled and is now an Administration Tower in all but name. As I write, the new Engineering building is preparing to dwarf Music, which has long since come down from the hill to join the campus spreading through the city. The functional utility of the Robbins era has been replaced with colourful cladding and great atriums, where prospective candidates can imagine their ideas soaring.

This new world is the result of education policy, which has emphasised the role of student choice and created an environment of institutional competition. New buildings all play a part in advertising the University as dream machine, capable of transforming student ambition and desire into employment and innovation, whilst producing the same world-class knowledge its reputation has been built on. I don't know much about comparable institutions but I imagine everywhere is much the same. I wonder what these bright, shiny, boastful buildings will look like in thirty years time, when I reach retirement age. I wonder whether I will work in one of these institutions and what I will do. Perhaps the future will look even brighter and even shinier.

The students walking between these buildings have changed in the time I've been at Sheffield. There are more international students, especially Asian students. There are pages on the University website written in Chinese. There are distance learning courses and degree programmes facilitated online, where the University maintains a huge presence, all designed according to its branding strategy. When I arrived in 2005 I didn't have a mobile phone. Maybe that was unusual then; it would be crazy now. The ideal researcher no longer hides in the office, writing and thinking, but blogs and tweets while they work, manifesting their personality alongside their ideas and interests. Appearances must appeal to prospective students and the public, an abstract public, that not only supplies students but is also served by the university and the knowledge it produces. This duty is made explicit by the funding regime: 20% of the Research Excellence Framework, the national system that proportions research funding, is decided on 'impact': a word that plots research communication like a ballistic field.

When I try to place this project—NO PICNIC—within the landscape I have sketched, I do so within this field of impact and public engagement. This is largely because of the role of artists in our project, which I equate with the developing role of artists in the research process embedded within this landscape.

Essentially, artists are good at making things look good. As such they have become more important to researchers during this period of change. It is believed that artists can help the public understand and appreciate the work of academics, who will then be rewarded by increased profile (which helps with attracting students) and better funding through the REF. It's a deal: artists get more work, academics engage their research to the public (who presumably benefit) = everyone's happy.

I try to convince myself that we wanted a project which would both subvert and critique this equation and therefore, somehow, subvert and critique the landscape it is embedded in, but I'm not sure that's quite true. We certainly wanted a project where the artists were integral to the research process and played a part in the decision making. As a result of this we didn't quite follow the research plan laid out in the proposal. Sandpit, the original name of the project, became an exploratory vehicle and we ranged widely. While ours was very much a communal drift, a group veering, it was definitely steered by the two artists who remained within the project. All this movement and uncertainty is definitely why we moved away from that name, Sandpit, which we all felt failed to communicate where we were heading. In the end, we decided on NO PICNIC. It's a better title, but one that we reached in the very last stages of the project.

What was wrong with Sandpit? Names and brands are essential to Higher Education's explicit market, and at base, sandpits are not meant to drift. They are human spaces, designed for controlled play. Sandpits are separate from the world, defined and limited, so that castles can be built in them and children can mess around. Sandpits are safe, don't hide any surprises and are sheltered from the elements. They are definitely not laboratories, where models of the world are constructed and tested. That is not to say that the laboratory had no place in our project. There was once a belief that the sandpit would lead to the lab. In part, this idea was adopted from the programme that provided our funding: the Sheffield Crucible. Nothing to do with the famous theatre, the Crucible is a model for encouraging interdisciplinary research adopted from the National Endowment for Science and the Arts. All of the researchers involved in the Sandpit were also members of the Sheffield Crucible. It's organised by Sandrine Soubes, the Researcher Development Manager for the Faculty of Science at the University of Sheffield.

In the Crucible a diverse group of researchers listened and talked to each other before coming up with projects, some of which were funded. Sandpit was one of those projects and an adaptation of the same model, one which introduced contemporary artists as the focus of collaboration. Why get researchers and artists to work together? One rationale comes from interdisciplinary research which believes that academic disciplines, while capable of great advances, also impose restraints, confining researchers into patterns of thinking. This is a bad thing because the world does not organise itself into academic disciplines. Because of this, the problems of mankind, whilst requiring specialists to understand aspects of them, also require specialists to work and think with specialists from other disciplines. Such collaboration is a form of speculative thinking, entertained to foster insight, maybe a breakthrough. Thus the laboratory was implicitly buried in our sand: one purpose of this odd group was to mutate, and by mutating produce new knowledge, or rather, test for the potential of new knowledge. If such a potential was confirmed, then our project, our sandpit, would lead to a larger funding bid, for proper money, from somewhere like the Arts & Humanities Research Council or NESTA itself.

While I'm sure all the participants would have appreciated more funding, there was something a little instrumental in this implied progression which conflicted with the open, exploratory nature of our engagement with each other. It reads well on paper, sensible even, but didn't feel right in practice. That's another reason why the name began to feel uncomfortable: sandpits are shallow things which you cannot sink into, safe places that have been assimilated into the assembly line process of funded research, places which refuse immeasurable and unquantifiable outcomes, places which must, by their nature, be justified by assessment. The sandpits of funded research demand a period of 'blue-sky thinking' before entering the lab. One cannot, like we did, remain in them, resisting the impulse to finish, sum-up, complete, produce. If anything this project became an oasis from the pressures of academia, a place that protected participants from the constant demands to be entrepreneurial, competitive, world-class, grant capturing, innovative, engaging, shiny, new.

Another reason why the name didn't stick is that sandpits are meant to be fun. Adults like to watch children mucking around in them. Sandpits make families happy. This association keyed in to a suspicion held by the group: that the project was funded because it provided a good show. Indeed, we were funded with the comment that 'real community engagement' should occur throughout the project. Initially, each element of our research proposal was designed to be public. Things didn't work out like that. The group blog wasn't publicised due to issues with opening Furnace Park. The public symposium happened without the public. One of the artists was meant to develop the project's ideas to be exhibited,

performed or sited in Furnace Park. Instead all six researchers incorporated artistic practice into their exploration of the wasteland, alongside, or at times led by, Bob and Hester. Nothing was built, exhibited or sited and 'the public' didn't really get a look in to the art/research process. And then we made this book.

I was responsible for running the thing, which is perhaps why I have fixated on names and drift, still suffering spikes of guilt for not following THE PLAN. A lot of this is ingrained. In my experience of funded academic research, you describe what you're going to do, do it, and then assess how well you did it. If things don't go to plan, you publish ignoring this. Precious little fails or deviates on paper. There's two reasons for this. Firstly, the pressure to be succinct and exact. Who has time for reading about dead ends when everything is about the results (the very ones that artists are meant to engage)? Secondly, there's the pressure to use one's funding efficiently and purposively, or else you might not get much research funding again.

So why did we drift? There was a general feeling that the collaborations were too early, too unformed, exploratory and delicate to engage the public. And that's assuming, of course, that 'the public' a) existed as a consistent and contiguous body (it doesn't) and b) that this non-existent body wanted to be engaged by a disparate group of researchers and artists (it didn't). On top of this there was that nagging sense that the first meaning of sandpit, a place to safely experiment, was undermined by the need for the results to be fun and accessible to outsiders, and that this was our 'real purpose': to perform for an audience. This unease is familiar to anyone who has worked on a public engagement project and was only thickened in the fresh air of Furnace Park, a place which necessarily gave our project a 'public face'.

Just like artists, researchers are increasingly having to perform. Why should they? Some are on precarious, temporary contracts and are paid to jig around. But the impulse to dance is also felt by full timers, derived from the market's focus on appearances and buried guilt over the hike in student fees, which has seen people pay for Higher Education twice over: as students on £9K a year and then again as taxpayers. There is much anxiety underneath the new, shiny, digital Sheffield.

The more a structure is subjected to market forces the more it becomes saturated by guilt. That's my theory. Just as the market maps desire onto buildings, it involves people in the personal manufacture of desire, where emotions become pointed, amplified, powerful. And that's just the staff! The students are even more anxious about developing and shaping their future. Everyone overproduces to compensate. It's all a bit like the rhythm & blues market in early 60s America. No one knew the formula to getting a hit record aside from the one that worked: release, release, release until the label gets a hit. Everything's done on a shoestring, none of the artists are paid properly, no one trusts each other and the songs are wracked with longing and frustration. That's not to say, of course, that the music isn't any good: there are frequent flashes of brilliance amongst the workmanlike material. Perhaps that's the market philosophy in a nutshell!

Did we shut the public out? Behave selfishly, arrogantly? Or wasn't there much for them to look at in the first place? Was it not arrogant of us to assume that we were hit makers? Perhaps, in the design of this project, we believed too much in artist-researcher collaboration as an engaging public process in and of itself. We meant well, wanting to break down that familiar formula of artists illustrating research findings. Or perhaps, in designing this project, we were simply playing the game of writing up the kind of project that funders want to fund. This meant positioning our interdisciplinary, researcher-artist collaboration as a) groundbreaking, b) full of potential, c) shiny and d) immediately accessible. Of course, it was not quite any of these things. But it got funded. And this book is that product, the output. It's not quite a product of the 'research plan'. The participants resisted the process of 'making' knowledge, just as they resisted the process of 'making' art. Perhaps it was ambitious to attempt this, especially when the participants were donating spare time not paid time.

As a result, the project, and to some extent the book has focused on process: the interaction between researchers and artists. At times this lost its binary orientation and became a group interaction. It was to this expanding state of practice that the participants willingly submitted, gradually turning away from attempts to communicate to 'the public' or indeed the research community. The act of recording the project in this book became a solution to some of the anxieties we experienced. A kind of postcard from the future, from a time when we understood what had occurred within the now-nameless sandpit. The book launch would be the artwork Sandpit had promised to deliver: the artists planned to hold a banquet at which everyone would give toasts and the book would be served up to the guests, who would all be drawn from the University and from those living around or close to Furnace Park. In doing so we hoped to envelop the guests within the process we had shared, to pass on whatever-this-project-was.

The proposal for this banquet is retained in this book. Due to a combination of reasons, practical and political, it never went ahead. Instead the participants held a breakfast of their own in Furnace Park, raising toasts to each other. It was rather nice. Yet, without anyone else, the project became even more personal, and this book grew in importance as an outcome beyond that. If anything, NO PICNIC has demonstrated, for me at least, that it is impossible to submit to a process such as artistic practice in a funded research project without attempting to communicate and thus justify findings, despite these findings being largely intangible or there being no one there to listen to them.

I have felt the resulting dissonance quite keenly when I have attempted to present this project, as if something had gone wrong and I wasn't sure what. Even this essay has taken many drafts and months to write, and I'm still anxious it says too little it too many words. Market forces must have saturated me! As a corollary, I suppose these could be early days for NO PICNIC in that the project might have an impact on my work and thinking beyond this book. Other people have said this elsewhere. And yet it might not: I may well find myself on to the next thing, or no thing. Of course, I'd like it to influence others, but it was such an effervescent process, I'm not sure these texts manage to comprehend it. Perhaps it is this sense of the intangible that is so very appealing to researchers at the moment, working as they are in a university becoming evermore explicit.

To demonstrate this strange, emotion saturated world, I wanted to illustrate this essay with images taken from the quicksand fetish scene which I discovered whilst looking up sandpits on the internet. The female protagonist is often clothed and always in peril. In many of the specialist videos she sinks until she is completely submerged. In some variants the protagonist might struggle and manage to escape; more often that not she submits to a simulated death, taking a certain pleasure from the experience. Instead of attempting to negotiate fair use of other people's pornography we have used a quicksand-related image from Britain. You will have to fill in the bodies, the peril, the excitement and the certain end, all documented for your ambivalent pleasure. The guilt comes later.

PARKLIFE

Hester Reeve

'Parks, their design, equipment and use', George Burnap, Philadelphia, Lippincott, 1916.

Indeed, in most advanced consumer societies the culture of political dissent seems lively and diverse. In the demonstration democracy (Etzioni, 1970) or social movement society (Meyer and Tarrow, 1998) non conventional forms of political articulation and participation have been fully normalized and belong to the standard repertoire of the most diverse social groups.

A banner in Gezi Park during Gezi Protests: 'Joy is Laughter of the Resistance'. Photo by Azirlazarus, 5th June 2013.

In this society post-conventional forms of political articulation and participation fulfill a new function: they represent an intra-societal physical and discursive space—the theme park—in which individuals, social groups and society at large can perform and experience key features of the traditional-modern condition which remain indispensable even though late-modern society has clearly moved beyond the traditional-modern phase.

'Parks, their design, equipment and use', George Burnap, Philadelphia, Lippincott, 1916.

In advanced capitalist consumer democracies the dominant strategy for this identity construction and self-experience is by means of acts of consumption. For obvious reasons, however, the hopes and expectations of the identity-seeking individual are constantly frustrated: acts of consumption can at best provide evidence of an already existing autonomous identity but they can never constitute one.

A few banners in Gezi Park during the protests: 'Silence the war and raise the peace', 'Listen Tell Hear Speak', 'Yes to peace', 'Those who responsible of Uludere shall be brought to justice'. Photo by Azirlazarus, 9th June 2013.

By reproducing the belief in the autonomous subject (voter) which supposedly is its external point of reference, the system of politics is in danger of reinforcing rather than resolving the problem: its promises heighten the horizon of expectations and, by implication, raise the potential for disappointment. In the effort to stabilize its own foundations, the system of politics may therefore even reinforce the experience of disempowerment and exclusion.

'Parks, their design, equipment and use', George Burnap, Philadelphia, Lippincott, 1916.

As the logic of the established system has permeated the very patterns of cognition and imagination of contemporary individuals, it is becoming increasingly difficult to even imagine a radically different society, let alone implement it. As late-modern individuals have fully embraced the patterns of identity construction offered by liberal consumer democracy, genuinely sustainable and globally just alternative models would, if really implemented, hardly be attractive or acceptable. It is probably safe to assume that despite their oppositional stance, even radical movement participants are in many respects rather fond of, and dependent on, the existing consumer culture.

View from Taksim Gezi Park. Photo by VickiPicture, 3rd June 2013.

Indeed, even Touraine, one of the founding fathers of New Social Movement theory, points out that while 'in the past, social movements were the embodiment of a project for a radical reconstruction of society and a figure of the Subject', contemporary protest movements have the 'sole objective' 'to create the Subject' (2000, p. 93), whereby the Subject is understood to mean 'the individual's effort to construct him or herself as an individual, rather than as a subordinate in a logic of order, whatever that order may be' (1992, p. 141).

'Parks, their design, equipment and use', George Burnap, Philadelphia, Lippincott, 1916.

From this perspective, the significance of social movement politics lies not so much in the demonstration of protest and opposition for the purpose of political change, but in the demonstration, performance and experience of something that is desperately needed in the late-modern condition but that has no place in the established socio-economic system: autonomy, identity, and agency.

2013 Taksim Gezi Park protests, a view from Taksim Gezi Park. Photo by VikiPicture 4th June 2013.

Social movements and other kinds of non-conventional political articulation can thus be interpreted as offering a supplementary form of identity construction which helps to compensate for the shortcomings of consumption-centred identity formation. They provide late-modern individuals with an opportunity to experience themselves both within (compliant with) and at the same time outside of (in opposition to, i.e. autonomous from) the system. Exactly this is required to escape the late-modern dilemma, and it is the unique characteristic and attractiveness of the theme park.

61

'Parks, their design, equipment and use', George Burnap, Philadelphia, Lippincott, 1916.

In the sense that the demonstration of autonomy, identity and political agency inside the theme park of radical action allows for full complicity with the status quo outside this arena, it may be described as a post-political and itself consumptive form of political articulation.

2013 Taksim Gezi Park protests, a view from Taksim Gezi Park. Photo by VikiPicture 3rd June 2013.

If it is correct to say, as suggested above, that the reproduction of the autonomous Self is not just a desire of late-modern individuals but a requirement for the self-reproduction of the increasingly one-dimensional system, social movements can thus be said to represent an essential resource for the stabilization of late-modern society. It would certainly be almost nonsensical to suggest that social movements explicitly intend to stabilize the established system. No empirical research would ever support such a claim. On the contrary, it would reveal that social movements not only explicitly want to challenge the system, but that they are actually successful in doing so.

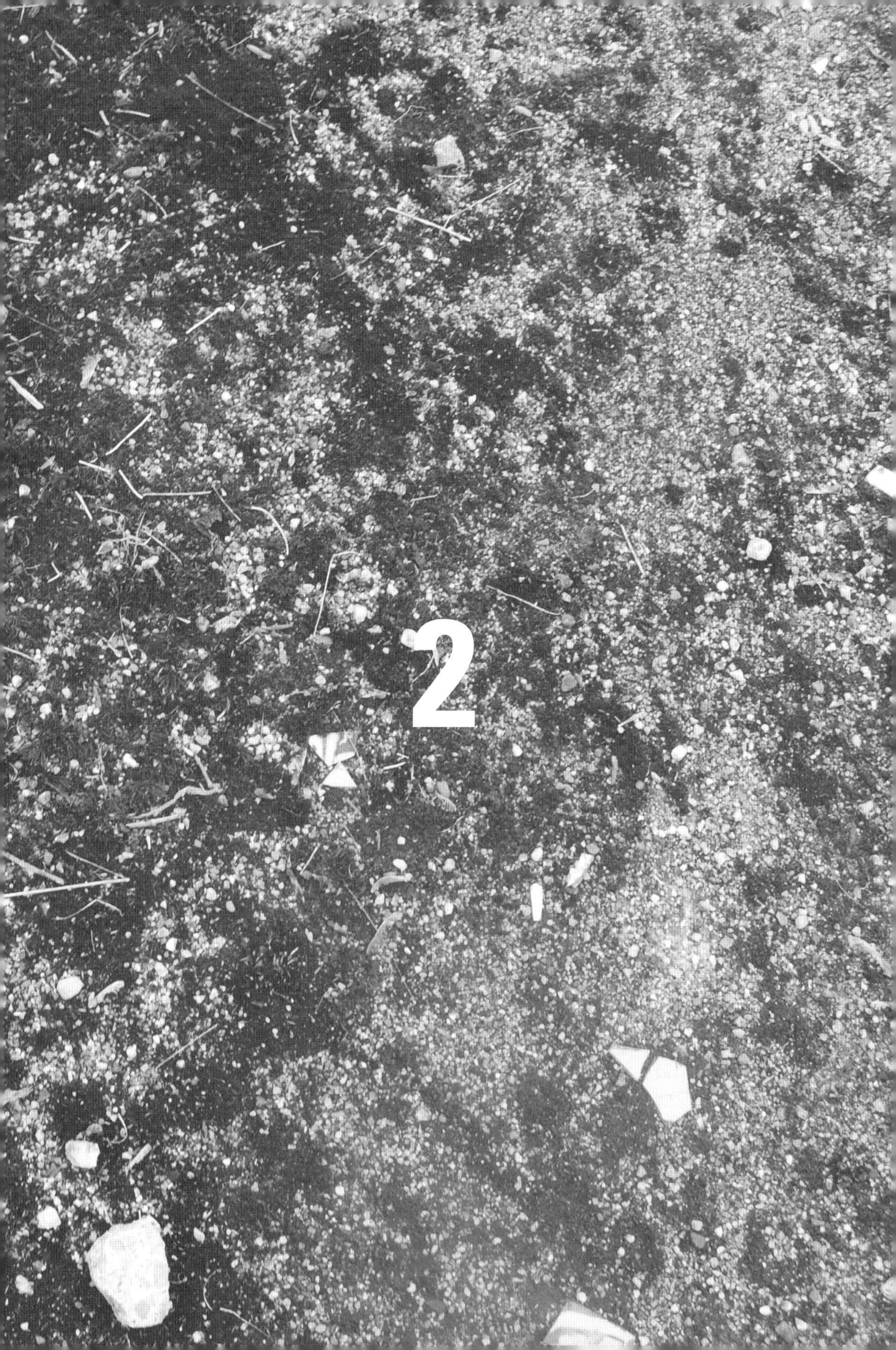
2

Curious…

Bob Levene

Hello Researchers,

Would you say you're more interested in what
is above the ground or below it?

Reply 1: Alison Beck

I often start by focusing on the details and moving on from there. In this picture I was drawn to the pipes underground that have been revealed. Earlier yesterday, I was talking to a student about his project to improve joints in water pipes (clean water, blue or yellow gas pipes... the one shown here is black, is that for dirty water? I must find out). I was wondering how to examine the joints in microscopic detail so he can work to improve them.

Reply 2: Bob Levene

The comforting smooth levels of resistance of that hip joint you showed was strangely satisfying. Its odd to think about the miles of wires and pipes around us as having joints, like some skeleton... that could move? I guess joints are the place of flexibility and motion but also weakness and vulnerability. The exposure of the pipes was the reason I took the photo. I'm curious about the hidden journey our 'living comforts' take before they conveniently pop out of a tap or turn on at a flick of a switch.

Reply 3: Arne Schröder

I can't say I know. I guess I am interested in all these things. Of course I study what is there, but what is there is only a part of what can be. Take the assemblage of plant species you see on the picture: why are there these species and not others? Why only a few individuals and not more? Because other species or individuals have not arrived yet? Why haven't they? Because they can't access the site? Why not? Aren't they there because the conditions are not conducive to their growth (too dry, too wet, too warm, too cold, too few insects for pollination, too many natural enemies eating their leaves, their roots?). Do the first plants keep out others by changing the local site to their benefit but to the detriment of others? Or no more species have evolved yet that can cope with such a habitat? I am actually quite surprised by myself now of what this picture, which I first found uninspiring, made me think about. Basically I covered the major questions of ecological theory here.

Reply 4: Bob Levene

Would we (humans) come into that analysis? I guess I mean how big is the picture you're looking at? The plants, the pipes, the brick, the soil etc. 'Pretty' pictures can be the most uninspiring of all.

Reply 5: Arne Schröder

Humans are part of the picture, but often quite implicit, in the background. Humans change the world and thus the environment of other species, but also their own environment. And indirectly, even moreso: changing how animals and plants live is coupled to the conditions of our existence. Ultimately, everything is connected and feedbacks are everywhere. Science often gets accused of being reductionistic, not holistic enough. I don't buy that. Of course we disassemble complex pictures into smaller, more handy and tractable bits. There is no other way if you want to understand things. But then these small bits are put together again, reassembling the big picture step by step, experiment by experiment, measurement by measurement, model by model. So at the end something emerges that is not the complete picture but a good approximation of the whole of it.

On science and arts

Arne Schröder

One reason why I joined this project was to learn and think more about how science and art work. I like to think that science is objective, analytical and dispassionate while in arts people are free to let their emotions and imagination run wild. The reason why I like this ideal distinction is that only then can I be sure that I don't fool myself when looking at the world through my models and my data, and moreover, only then can I trust other people's conclusions about how a particular piece of the world works. I also like that because it gives me freedom when appreciating art: I can more justify any personal and subjective feeling I get when doing so, instead of being patronised by someone into a certain way of interpretation or thinking. The problem with this, though, is that this distinction is not correct. It is very wrong. I always knew that, but this project helped me realise that even more sharply.

For scientists, a lot of emotion goes into how we choose projects, we feel deeply about our theories and data, their value for understanding and more. I don't say that is necessarily a bad thing: compassion, creativity and imagination are needed to come up with novel, maybe more promising approaches, and help get over that constant feeling of stupidity so common when doing research. They are also the stuff that keep you going when calculations fail, test animals die, equipment breaks, money stops flowing... However, it makes the rest of science (experimentation, sample protocols, measuring stuff, calculations) a constant struggle to fight yourself (and other scientists) to not give in to wishful thinking, to not bias yourself towards certain pet conclusions, etc.

Tim's work gave me further insights. Through his moving machines and when talking to him last Friday I became aware that art projects often also have to be precise and analytical to get messages across, to take material and physical/biological constraints into account but also to use chances offered by new technology (everybody loved the artificial metallic hip joint Allison brought along as a demonstration object).

Or look at Bob's work on subjective feelings regarding the flow of time and the perception of space. I guess she needed to contrast that with actual scientific measurements of time and space to get at the discrepancy between objective, machine-based measurements and subjective, human feelings. On the other hand, as a biologist I would say that these can't be too much off. People still are able to make it in the real world without getting lost. Evolution saw to that.

Reply 1: Matthew Cheeseman

Really interesting post. To pick one thing out of it:

>>They are also the stuff that keeps you going when calculations fail, test animals die, equipment breaks, money stops flowing.

Two things that interest me: 1) Much of our lives as scientists and artists are effected by chance, meeting people, exchanging ideas, saying things, overhearing things, reading things that somehow cross your path. I often think that a body of work is in contravention to all of these things that bubble and provoke us. One has to be very persistent to keep a route through all the fascinating things life throws at us. 2) At the same time much of our life is ruled by deep structures we have little understanding or influence over. Economy. Class. Media.

This indeed is one of the fundamental sociological problems: what is the relationship between a) individual agency and b) structural position. Your answer to that is embedded within your politics.

Material matters

Bob Levene

Reply 1: Caroline Evans

These are images of material provided by Roxspur?

Reply 2: Matthew Cheeseman

They're not, I don't think. I find the first very disturbing.

Reply 3: Bob Levene

No, these are images I took whilst visiting Jonathan's and Alison's departments on Friday.

I like these two. The man in black is Garry Wiggins, the University's surveyor, the man in a High Visibility Jacket is Brad Hurt from Roxpur. Both were charging around Furnace Park on the day that you all met and had the tour. In the picture they are assessing boundaries. I am thinking back to how I walked you around in a very guided fashion, as someone said, a bit like a school teacher. This seemed like the right thing to do: collaborations without set aims are awkward, are they not? They need structure. This puts in mind Sarah's post on Sunday, about occupying the space, understanding a relation to it, a purpose.

Reply 1: Sarah Spencer

I keep thinking about
when I turned up at the

Classical inspiration

Hester Reeve

I keep thinking about those two old lumps of cement lying menacingly in the top part of the park, they look like they fell from the top of a very thick wall. They also look like archeological remnants. I like the way they are heavy, but they are a bit ugly and also there to stay. It's made me think about a real archeological site in Turkey, Diogenes' famous wall (a great example of ideas grown in the city centre):

'Diogenes of Oenoanda was an Epicurean Greek from the 2nd century AD who carved a summary of the philosophy of Epicurus onto a portico wall in the ancient city of Oenoanda in Lycia (modern day southwest Turkey). The surviving fragments of the wall, which originally extended about 80 meters, form an important source of Epicurean philosophy. The inscription sets out Epicurus' teachings on physics, epistemology, and ethics. It was originally about 25000 words along and filled 260 square meters of wall space. Diogenes built the wall so that all the citizens of his town could learn and be inspired from it. He said if there were one or two people that were lost he could educate them personally. But there are many. So he decided to put up the wall. According to Epicurus, in order to live wisely, it isn't enough to read a philosophical argument once or twice, we need constant reminders of it or we'll forget.'

Quotes taken from: en.wikipedia.org/wiki/Diogenes_of_Oenoanda

Currently, about a quarter of the inscription—in fragments spread across the terrain—has been recovered. The inscriptions contains three treatises written by Diogenes as well as various letters and maxims:

'A Treatise on Ethics, which describes how pleasure is the end of life; how virtue is a means to achieve it; and explains how to achieve the happy life.

A Treatise on Physics, which has many parallels with Lucretius, and includes discussions on dreams, the gods, and contains an account of the origin of humans and the invention of clothing, speech and writing.

A Treatise on Old Age, which appears to have defended old age against the jibes of the young, although little of this treatise survives.

Letters from Diogenes to his friends, which includes a letter addressed to a certain Antipater concerning the Epicurean doctrine of innumerable worlds.

Epicurean maxims, a collection of the sayings of Epicurus and other eminent Epicureans, which was appended to the end of the treatise on ethics.

Letters of Epicurus, which includes a letter to Epicurus' mother on the subject of dreams.'

Reply 1: Sarah Spencer

I think I agree with that Epicurus about constant reminders. Also think I could do with reading that treatise on ethics. Like the idea of a rough concrete rebellion in Furnace Park, determined to stay put, nagging and niggling, about some forgotten industrial lesson learned.

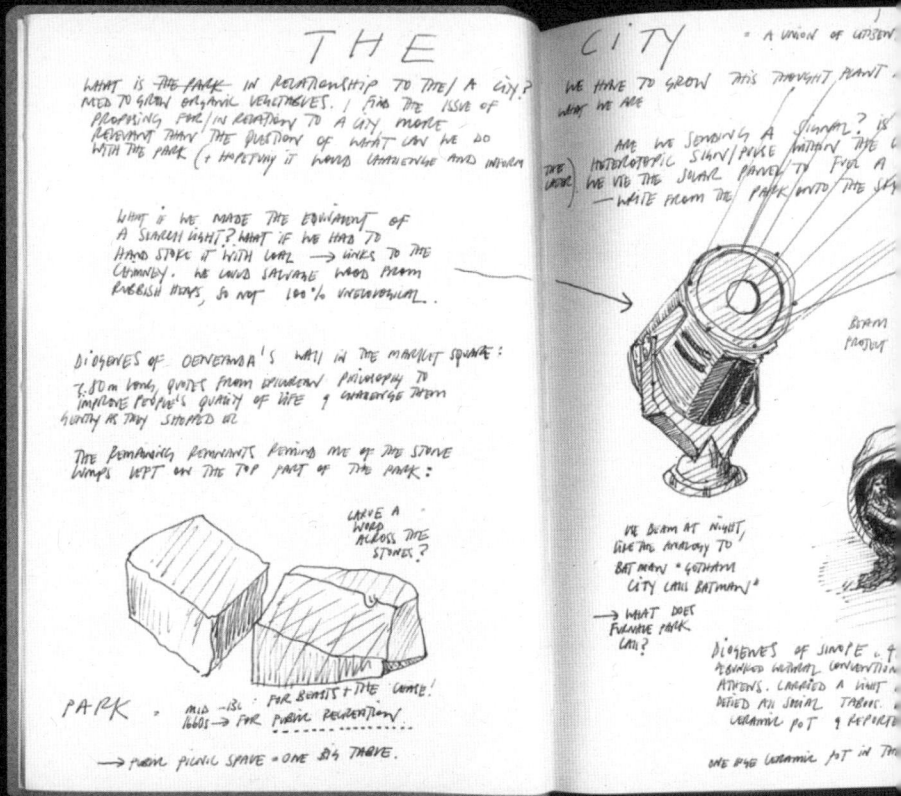

Many ways of how nature acts as a sculptor

Arne Schröder

Humans have created sculptures for at least 40,000 years. One of the oldest pieces of art is the Venus vom Hohle Fels, a small female figurine carved out of mammoth ivory. If you see humans as an integral part of nature (and I believe that despite all our technology we are still, and probably always will be, part of the biosphere on Earth), this is one indirect way of nature acting as a sculptor.

I work with animals that can be highly plastic in the way they look, behave, operate, etc. So another way nature acts as a sculptor is through evolution and ecology. I am also a passionate rambler and hiker and I have seen landscapes and structures, like arctic tundra and rock formations that are sculpted by yet other forces. What do you think? Are these different ways somehow linked by the actions of natural forces (note that I don't want to anthropomorphise them even if I speak here of nature as a sculpturing subject) or is this just superficial and coincidence?

For example, the joint forces of evolution and ecology led to different body forms in two individuals of the same species of water fleas. One individual was exposed to predator cues, while the other grew up in a predator-free environment.

A page from my sketch book

Hester Reeve

Reply 1: Alison Beck

Thanks for showing the page from your notebook. It makes me want to start an illustrated notebook of my own! My work notebooks mainly contain written notes e.g. lab notes and only have a few 'sketches' of equipment to help me remember how to use them. The use of solar power (once suitably stored, as described in another strand) to project images (at night?) is intriguing.

Reply 1: Hester Reeve

Even my stomach responded to this stimulating post (I mean it made my stomach think so to speak)... that's almost a metaphor of nature sculpting, but in this case my emotions.

I totally agree, nature is carving all the time. I am never sure if this means we should co-carve with her/him/it? Perhaps to find things out, but does it make sense to carve with her in order to achieve beauty? I know you were not suggesting that, but it's an interesting issue. Does it change us? What if the sculpted form of the water flea exposed to predators is more beautiful, more extraordinary to my human 'sense of taste/'rightness' than the one who stayed 'safe'? I'm someone who can't watch the lions hunting the zebras etc. I get absolutely upset.

Did you see the program about the art of the ice age? It was very good, and talks a little about some of this (the forms 'carved using flint and out of flint' took ages... so experts now think that certain humans were 'artists' in that this was their role and they didn't hunt or gather all those eons ago... But I don't want to end this post on 'artists'... so I'll end it paying tribute to the beauty of the water flea.

Scratching the surface

Bob Levene

Visiting Alison and Jonathan in their prospective engineering labs last Friday has left me with that exciting but frustrating feeling I get some times when I'm at the beginning of something, unable to articulate why and what it is that I'm excited about. For sometime I've been drawn to the (admittedly broad) areas of engineering, infrastructure and materials. Possibly because they seem to bring together interests such as resources, environment, technology, geopolitics, economics, but some how routed in the practical, the day to day, the mundane, the human as well as somehow commenting or exposing how we like to live and function.

There is something about it that is inherently sculptural, not just in the forms and objects created (with aesthetic decisions being made alongside or often following function), but also in the systems and networks we've created to feed, heat, communicate and transport ourselves. Alison's research looks at the surface of materials and was fascinating to learn about. Using different methods (optical, electron, laser) to analyse, 'see' and understand the surface as whole. Rubbing, scratching, hammering again and again, testing the mettle so to speak. Creating, coating, changing the surface chemistry, maybe only a few microns thick to make it more resistant or reduce friction, maybe better for growing cells in bioengineering or be less corrosive for medical devices, maybe more durable for turbine blades.

Surfaces, even the shallowest ones, seem to have a lot to them after all. It's the front line, the edge, the point of contact, the touch, the skin, the barrier, the protector, the mirror, the image, the language. I like the potential of scratching the surface,

embedding, scarring and marking. I explored this idea in a previous worked called Handmade. My work as a photographer is defined by 'managing surfaces' describing objects by the way you light and create reflections on them.

Whilst walking around the lab I was particularly taken by these small sweet like, appealing objects that turned out to be test samples. Slices of a material are embedded into resin and polished in order to fix them into place ready to be put under a microscope. Depending on the type of material and the form it comes in, a different surface pattern is created. I'd like to study, photograph, look at these objects and other processes the material goes through further.

The afternoon with Jonathan and his colleagues opened up a different scale and loads of thinking. The railways were the topic of discussion, maintaining 5,000 miles of track, keeping leaves off the line, stopping sand from corroding the wheels, risk vs. safety vs. money. There seemed to be crossovers with Alison's research in the resistance and resilience of material surfaces. The wheels on the track for one: Jonathan talked about the beuracracy and rules Network Rail have in place dictating the various strengths of steel that should be used for train wheels. Too strong and they wear the track down, but the longer they last for the company that runs the train.

It's the enormity of it all that fascinates me, transport, be it moving us or our water, heat, conversation, pictures. Infrastructure can be thought of as the loom on which we weave the very fabric of our lives, enabling us to move freely, consume, communicate, keep warm and fed; for most of us it is only something

we become aware of when it goes wrong. These networks tie us into global systems, yet we rarely see beyond the switch, tap or aisle of food on our doorsteps, but our lives are vulnerable to the economic and geopolitical situations that arise across the world. I'm left thinking about the material (raw/surface), the surface, the scale and distance, the connections and networks.

Reply 1: Caroline Evans

Scale, distance, the connection and networks are all very interesting and relevant to the function of cells: components of life from the unicellular to multicellular. Feels like these themes form patterns which are repeated across the project.

Reply 2: Alison Beck

I'm going to cut up ('section') some pieces of coated steel in a few minutes. I will then be able to analyse the sections in a variety of ways; from the macroscopic to microscopic, physical and chemical properties. Bob, you are welcome to take more photos of these and other processes.

Subnature

Alasdair Hiscock

As I've read through everything that's been posted, I think two themes have stood out so far.

One is the theme of surface and structure. We've seen ideas of surface markings in the landscape; the surface of materials and minute changes to their properties; the uncovering of infrastructures under the surface; the suggestion that our lives play out as surface detail of a huge network, but how this idea works at the level of tiny cells too; how the natural world sculpts and shapes; trying to preserve an area of the site during the process of development.

The other idea that comes across strongly is about language, and the production of things. How language is used to assert a place in the world; the problem of discussing 'nature' from a perspective of recreating it; a very particular type of language used in site surveys, one that doesn't accept any contingency whatsoever; a quite useful distinction between analysis and emotion when we talk about art and science.

These seem linked for me, in the way that across every type of work there's always a need to exclude certain ideas or possibilities in order to make progress. In art, design, writing, scientific research, etc.

This brought to mind an interesting book/project by the architectural historian David Gissen. He proposes the idea of 'subnature' in contrast to 'seemingly central and desirable forms of nature e.g. the sun, clouds, trees and wind'. In particular, he wants to propose an alternative to the instrumentalisation of nature in architecture—contemporary 'green' architecture being 'the utilisation of nature as an instrument that cleans the world, increases productivity and efficiency, and transforms our existing natural relationship, while advancing the social sphere as is'.

Subnatures are the marginalised and disregarded side of natural life, such as mud, weeds, dust and pigeons. They are fought against, not seen as the good natures that can provide us with help. However, as the book explores, they can and have been accommodated into the planning of buildings and everyday life through history. This doesn't apply specifically to the Furnace Park site, but I thought it was an interesting point to explore, when we have discussed ecology, materials engineering, the representation of natural beings and indeed the most green of green things—solar power for the site.

So, where's this all going? What I'm coming to is the idea that all work excludes certain things, indeed it tries to not change certain factors. In every project, there's a possible outcome with terrible consequences that we have to avoid, or we don't know is there. I'm tempted, as a non-scientist, to imagine that this catastrophe scenario is always there in scientific research, as if an accidental turn in the laboratory could immediately destroy the world.

What I'd like to know is what element of your work might be described as 'subnatural'? Perhaps something that is genuinely undesirable that has to be suppressed, or a possible consequence that concerns you. This could be something that you do in your everyday work, or something that has come up in the course of this collaboration. Essentially, I want to know what the thing is that is the opposite of what you're actually trying to achieve?

Ideas post
Alasdair's post

Hester Reeve

This was a very thought provoking post, and timely. It's tied some things together and given me some ideas for something to do in the park but I share this as an offering and not a demand that we should do any of it (well, we should, but it may be too far fetched!):

In terms of surfaces, I am taken by the idea of each of us scratching the surface as we traverse the park… which has been untrodden by human foot for so long… so our very walking across it is somehow a 'thing' and 'artful' in its own right. Not that I/we have been there so many times. This makes me want to spend a 24-hour period in Furnace Park constantly walking around and across the space, ideally with the whole group there… a marathon of sorts but as much a marathon of conversation— if the whole group were doing this we could have megaphones and hold a conversation together as we traverse on our own random pathways through the space. There is an echo here of ancient practices of philosophy too (carried out in groups walking rather than via texts in books). This would be interesting for others to pop in and watch/listen, but more importantly would actually facilitate concerns and ideas between us because it would stretch what a shared conversation can be, it would remove the politeness and constraints on our ability to think together outside the box. We would be sorting something out rather than showing a conclusion. I also like the way this ties in with the equivalence with a cell (and I haven't posted about cells but I was fascinated by everything that has been said in relation to that). I like the way that if we did this walking performance event and recast Furnace Park as the (rebel) cell of the 'city body,' then our traversing to and fro would be like DNA moving within the cell, carrying/creating messages. Alison's 'golden scissors' could play a role here—if viewed within the same metaphor of the ark as a cell, then these scissors are like a chromosome, a chromosome of potentiality. We could pass the scissors between us as we talk... or hand them to one another as an invitation to talk. Of course we could take breaks, eat etc. but I like the commitment to at least twelve hours doing this.

Linked to this are other ideas. I have been pondering about how hard it seems to get to what we could make/what we could do in the park and how to link all of our interests related so far. It makes you feel precious (even though Matt has always given us the freedom to do or not to do etc.). So, during the blog period, I've found myself sitting at my lap top but rather than knowing what to post, I've found that my imagination just keeps going back to the park, like quite viscerally in that the colours are vivid and I can feel the cold and the emptiness and am always happy to turn and see the furnace chimney out the corner of my eye etc. So, my strongest sense during the research period is that I have been waiting in the park all this time. I'm cold but I don't want to leave. Now I am getting this image of those really evocative wooden bus shelters (why on earth do they not build those anymore? Why do they take away those ornate city lamps and put an awful piece of public art in the city centre instead? Can we salvage an ornate lamp-post and put it in the park? Fueled by the solar panels?). I have a strong image of about ten of these wooden bus shelters around the edge of the performance area of the park. They would serve the useful function of shelter for any audiences to future events, they set up a stage as it were (non-traditionally) but most of all they run counter to the idea of linear progression/journey since they are arranged facing each other in a large rectangle shape, and suggest a waiting/hope for the future.

But what I was really asked to think about was what is the opposite of what I am trying to achieve? The thing I am not trying to do is to repeat the problem of public art projects(!) where usually ugly/uncomfortable artworks are made as a type of service provision and equated with progress and value. It's patronizing to people and to art. For me the best cities are ones where children can go scrambling in open fields or play on streets in total safety and you don't need an Arts Council grant or an artist for that. So, I am trying not to place an 'art object' in the park. I am also not doing anything technological but that is because I am not very good at engineering type things... So, whilst this is opposite to what I am thinking about so far, this is something I would love the challenge of doing and I'm thinking of those solar panels and Tim's adeptness with building machines. I'm all up for putting a machine (which I interpret very broadly, even ideas can be machines of sorts for me) in the park, solar powered. But I wouldn't know where to start and that's quite exciting.

I'm also attaching a drawing I just made from a photograph of 'The People's Militia' training in Victoria Park, London, c.1913. It was organized by Sylvia Pankhurst's East London Federation of Suffragettes. I'm not suggesting we form an army (well, it could be fun, we could make an equivalent of guns that sowed seeds everywhere or were in fact musical instruments that we could play), but it's such a great 'non-park park' image (possibly subnature-ish too), expectant, rebellious and committed.

Destruction and creation

Jonathan Paragreen

I am fascinated by the discussions which are going on here and having had a busy couple of weeks am catching up. And have had a couple of thoughts below.

Hester's post reminded me of the inscriptions in the stone at the Cow and Calf near Ilkley. I remember when I first saw these inscriptions about 17 years ago I was unsure whether to consider them art or more as graffiti with the negative feelings of destruction which go with that.

However, I like the idea of art forming one thing, but in the process destroying something else. For the inscriptions to have been made at the Cow and Calf both stone surface and the chisel will have been worn in order to create this (I like how this relates to the research areas of wear and the science of surfaces).

In the video of Tim's sculpture (where you turn the handle and it writes out the word love), the pencil made a horrible squealing sound, which reminds us that the pencil is being worn in order to create the words and ultimately will be destroyed. Bob is fascinated by infrastructure, but again roads, railways, gas pipelines, power cables all remind me of the arguments which are always raised in planning about them destroying the existing landscape: we require the services they bring but we need to destroy a landscape to achieve them. Even as I am writing this, I have started to consider that the power my PC requires has probably come from a coal or gas power station, the extraction of these sources of energy have also resulted in destruction of landscapes or marine habitats. Hester asked why we don't have wooden bus shelters and my first thought was, cost and secondly the susceptibility to vandalism and destruction. Also more abstractly from Hester's post showing the 'The People's Militia' training in Victoria Park, London, this again reminded me that in order to create universal suffrage, many lives were destroyed and sacrifices made.

Sarah's work with vocabulary and how different sections of society manage equally well with less vocabulary or different vocabulary made me consider that perhaps education and common language also destroys something in society. I don't believe that any of these things are not right or worthwhile, just that all the time we are losing something to make something. And linking to Arne's work, I am sure that evolution is about loss as well gain, often losing the ability to do something which is now unnecessary and gaining other evolutionary advantages.

So how does this relate back to Furnace Park? I like the idea that we can celebrate the cycles of creation and destruction the park has already gone: from woodland to agricultural to industrial, which has now decayed to what it is today. I have a vision of a sculpture by Tim which is grinding away at the concrete floor either representing the mining or such industries destroying the landscapes, or even wearing an inscription into the concrete and showing the destruction of the ground and the tool over time. I can imagine Bob and Hester capturing other losses and destructions, perhaps Hester the losses and gains of political and historical struggles and Bob capturing some of her insights into modern infrastructure and the

contrasts between what that brings and destroys. I feel that the park itself can also be a representation of this with existing trees and perhaps some grass and meadow flowers planted and perhaps even vegetable crops planted to represent the different eras of the site and what has been destroyed to create it.

Reply 1: Hester Reeve

100 yesses to all of the above, very inspiring. It would be great to have one of Tim's machines grinding a word into the surface of the concrete. I wonder if that would deter graffiti on the bus shelters (destruction leading back to creative force?). Maybe his machine could be scribing a statement about people's struggles and the destruction/creation therein (but for the record, the suffragettes never hurt a living thing save the king's horse at the Derby, which was an accident and he survived).

Reply 2: Bob Levene

Your thoughtful and considered post makes me think about the cycle of things, it also brings up thoughts around time and balance. Is there an evenness or balance to this pattern of creation and destruction? Does there need to be? What if the scales tip? It reminded me of the cables and guides on the top of trains and the wheel and tracks below, which all wear down at different rates. When two things come up against each other something has to give. What matter, attitude, technique, composition survives longer; strength, density, resilience, flexibility/agility, resistance, reproduction or refresh. As Caroline explained to me this morning when describing what cells do: survive grow develop or die?

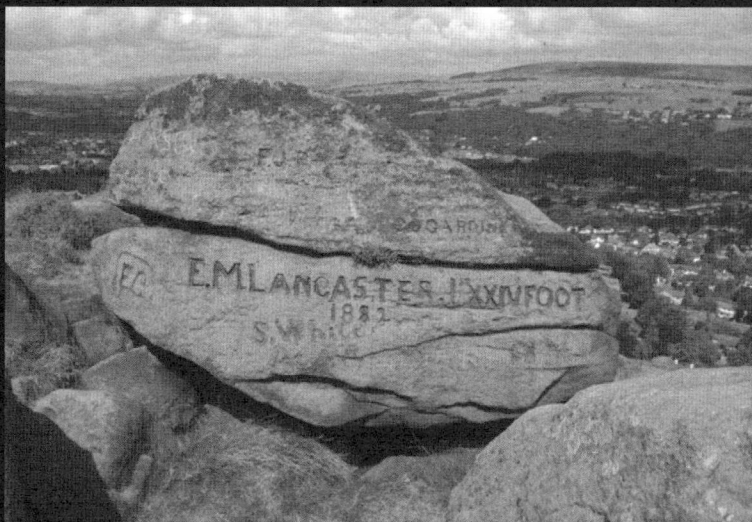

The destructor

Alison Beck

Hester's 'ideas-post-Alasdair's-post' has sparked some connections for me (networks of cells/neurones as mentioned by Caroline in another post?) concerning gas lamps in Sheffield. When I moved to a hill in Sheffield (towards the end of the last century) there was one beautiful, ornate gas lamp on the hill which was actually lit, and it burned day and night. I thought this was a wonderful and romantic gesture, there to remind us of how it was when Sheffield was lit by gas lamps. Several months later, I carefully read the grimy letters around the base of the lamp:

SEWER GAS DESTRUCTOR

How my illusions were shattered! There are several of these 'gas lamps' in Sheffield, as far as I know they are no longer lit. So it begs the question what happens to the pockets of sewer gas (methane?) that used to form in sewers of hilly regions like Sheffield. I will ask a friend whose research includes waste water!

There is a lot more to think about. I like Hester's idea of 'walking and talking' and the links to our past, more on these areas later.

Reply 1: Bob Levene

I love that it's a SEWER GAS DESTRUCTOR.

This is taken from 'The History of Monkseaton Village' by local historian Charlie Steel found on the English Heritage website:

'In the 1890s, Joseph Edmund Webb, a builder from Birmingham, invented and patented his sewer gas destructor lamp, and later formed the Webb Engineering Company. Within ten years of their introduction, these lamps were found all over England and in many other parts of the world. Old sewers were often badly laid out and poorly vented, so there was always a danger of disease (or even explosion) from methane and fetid stagnant gases, which could build up in the system. The lamps, which were connected to the ordinary town gas supply, were installed at high points in the system and were coupled directly to the underground sewer. They were usually lit by three mantles, which were rarely extinguished. The burning mantles created an intense heat within the hood, leading to an updraught, which drew air from the sewer through a copper tube inside the column; the sewer gas was therefore harmlessly burned off, thus converting the methane into carbon dioxide before being released into the atmosphere. One lamp was capable of venting an area of up to three quarters of a mile of sewer.'

Reply 2: Alison Beck

Thanks for adding that excellent description Bob. I had a brief chat about the sewer gas destructors with my friend and fellow researcher, Will Shepherd who is based in the Pennine Water Group, Department of Civil and Structural Engineering. I asked him if he had any ideas why the old sewer gas destructor lamps around Sheffield were not lit any more. Whilst this is well to the side of his main research area he made some interesting comments which I would like to share:

'I've worked with sewers for over 10 years and had never come across sewer gas destructors! I would guess that more efficient methods of venting sewers have been developed and perhaps an increased understanding of the problem has negated the need (odour is a nuisance, not a health hazard). As far as I can make out, these were essentially gas lamps running initially on town gas and later natural gas. The heat was supposed to provide an airflow to remove the gas and anything combustible would be burnt. I think in general stack pipes provide sufficient airflow through the systems for it not to be a problem. The main gas issue in sewers is hydrogen sulphide. I'm not aware that methane is a major issue, other problems are odour related. Hydrogen Sulphide is mainly a problem in tanks and where the sewer is stationary for long periods, e.g. pumped mains, creating odours, causing corrosion and being potentially fatal to people entering the sewer, which is why they always use gas monitors.

I also wonder if increased flow in the sewerage systems might make a difference in some parts. We are using the same pipes as when they were installed, but there are more houses and larger paved areas. This leads to greater flows, which are likely to be at higher velocities resulting in less sediment deposition. This could mean that there is less degradation of the sewage in the pipes and with smaller quantities of gases produced?'

The right to land

Bob Levene

Excited by the recent entries by Alisdair and Hester, below is my response. Although I want to pre-empt it with saying how I'm still unsure about resolving, or making comment/or work so soon and for the sake of it. To me it feels like the conversation is only just getting started. Having said that…

I find the notion of subnature an interesting one, how we give a hierarchy to nature based on our own understanding of beauty. Placing importance on the dramatic, bleak and cute over the seemingly dull, odd and mundane. Do we only try to manage and use nature for our own sake? Giving importance and focus to that which we find aesthetically pleasing, useful and productive? I can understand the desire to, as Arne said 'greening' sites such as Furnace Park, which no doubt has a lot of value to it, but I wonder if revealing, exposing, uncovering, discussing and making aware of what already exists has its own value.

Sewer gas destructor lamps remove sewer gases and their hazards. That is pretty exciting for me, it somehow brings together interests around infrastructure and the power and energy we use. I like the idea of an alternative physical manifestation or indicator of used energy and a connection between the hidden infrastructure below the surface and a visible signifier above.

Hesters idea of live, temporal shared conversations is a beautiful one as is a long duration of time spent in the park. There is something about the temporal, democratic notion of open dialogue in relation to the more permanent public carved wall of philosophy or the wear and tear markings in the landscape. It also links to Jonathan's ideas of losing something to make something and Hester's idea of sorting something out rather than concluding with a neat finish.

Maybe this could be an alternative approach to the symposium? A durational open dialogue/set of performances/actions on site.

Finally, Sarah mentioned something in an earlier post about the power of looking closely that somehow resonated with me that I wanted to re-post: 'We examine our surrounding reality, we attend to its details and sometime through looking closely we make it appear strange'.

Reply 1: Sarah Spencer

Really interested in the idea of 'giving importance and focus to that which we find aesthetically pleasing, useful and productive' I also wonder 'if revealing, exposing, uncovering, discussing and making aware of what already exists has its own value'.

Small bubbles

Bob Levene

Today I visited Arne and his water fleas. It was a lot to take in and the conversation got pretty broad and included ideas around truth and truths; a scientific truth being something that had proof and was evidence based and repeatable. Why is this truth any more truthful than others? How these experiments are small controlled and isolated bubbles in a bigger pond.

I got to look at a water flea and a baby water flea feeding through a microscope, which was quite a sight, a transparent shell with a clear pumping heart and brown tube which looked like a spine, but turned out to be its gut. The thing that Arne said that stuck with me most was about how the rate of dispersal or transfer of species has changed and increased since humans have become more globalised.

We talked about how small and microbiotic creatures get onto cargo ships when they fill up with ballast water, despite filters and netting designed to prevent this. When the ships travel to the other side of the world and offload the ballast water and reload cargo, they release foreign species which 'invade' and sometimes destroy the local ecosystem.

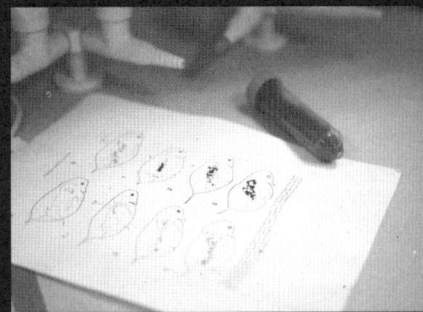

Survive grow develop or die

Bob Levene

This will be my fourth lab visit and I'm beginning to notice each has a particular subtle smell, not to mention beautiful displays of glass bottles and odd things in fridges. Visiting Caroline in the processing lab felt strangely familiar, partly because they develop protein samples on gels, which is not too dissimilar to the photographic process.

We talked about her fascinating work on analysing and breaking down proteins. I also got a well needed lesson in what cells do and how they work. This led to a discussion around knowledge and the feeling of knowing less the more you learn. When isolating environments and conditions to see what happens (as so many lab based sciences do), there almost seems a compulsion and need to known more. The question came up: in order to help, mend and discover are we then creating more problems? It reminds me of the discussions around creation and destruction that are being blogged.

I'm pretty taken aback at how broad engineering is and even more interested in how aspects crossover. Although it makes sense when I looked at the dictionary definition of engineering: 'the art or science of making practical application of the knowledge of pure sciences, as physics or chemistry, as in the construction of engines, bridges, buildings, mines, ships, and chemical plants'. It does look like the examples need updating, as the University departments within the Faculty of Engineering include Aerospace, Automatic Control and Systems, Bioengineering, Chemical and Biological Engineering, Civil and Structural Engineering, Computer Science, Electronic and Electrical Engineering, Materials Science and Mechanical Engineering.

Reply 1: Caroline Evans

Thanks to Bob for paying a visit which encompassed a tour of a lab in the Medical School and then on to the ChELSI labs in Chemical and Biological Engineering. Would like to extend this invitation to others too. We talked for a couple of hours and the time just flew. As Bob said 'The question came up; in order to help, mend and discover are we then creating more problems?' We discussed that recent posts by Alison and Jonathan deal very effectively with this and this all relates back to Alisdair's subnature blog which has provoked a series of interesting responses. We talked about the post on hexagram and Bob said it reminded her of the exhibition 'Forms' by Quayola and Memo Atken in Bradford, 2012, which is a very beautiful analysis of human movement.

Hester's comment that 'In terms of surfaces, I am taken by the idea of each of us scratching the surface as we traverse the park... which has been untrodden by human foot for so long... so our very walking across it is somehow a "thing" and "artful" in its own right' led to discussion that historical aspects of the space remain to be addressed. I was particulary taken with Tim's initial thought to use railings to fence off a few square meters of the middle of the lower area and keep that bit untouched from any site improvement and as it is now. For the reasons of 1) Preserving the initial starting point, 2) As a kind of spurious control sample to compare to whatever the site becomes and 3) Just curiosity as to how the site develops. We also discussed that immersion in thinking about a project is a powerful creative force, particularly in conversation and whether Hester's suggestion to spend some time walking around the site in conversation could be a very productive and complementary activity to the blogs to date.

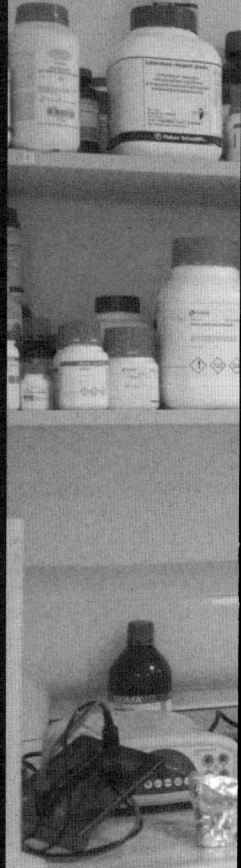

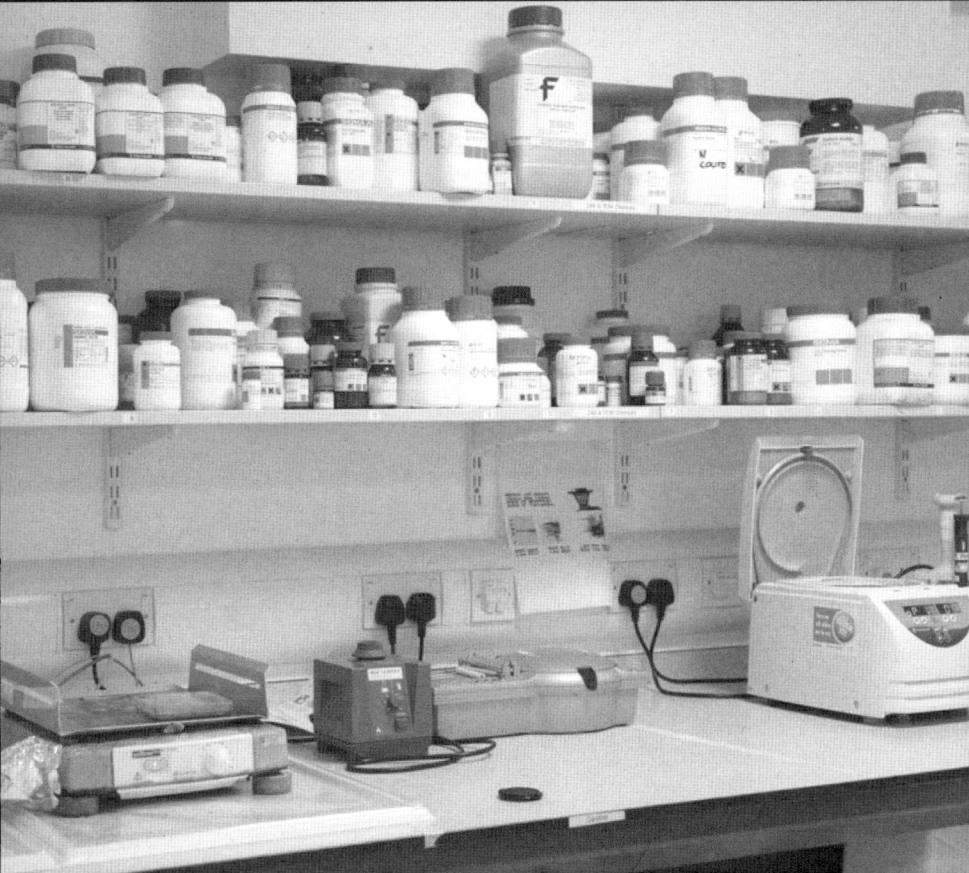

Infrastructure

Caroline Evans

Decided to blog about infrastructure as this has emerged in conversation with Bob. What is meant by infrastructure? The Oxford English Dictionary defines this as 'the basic physical and organizational structures and facilities (e.g. buildings, roads, power supplies) needed for the operation of a society or enterprise'.

On a more personal level, in terms of my research areas of cell biology, biochemistry and chemical engineering and approaches used to explore this: what do I understand this to mean? The infrastructure of eukaryotic (including human) cells is provided by the cytoskeleton. It is clear also that infrastructure is highly applicable to many areas including engineering which encompasses a number of areas as discussed previously by Bob in her blog in

Carbon Coating

Bob Levene

Reply 1: Alison Beck

These pictures, taken by Bob, show some of the diverse sample preparation for scanning electron microscopy (SEM). One project in Materials Science and Engineering is studying low friction coatings on steel and the other (jointly with Mechanical Engineering) is to improve joints in plastic pipelines (mentioned in an earlier post of mine). The insulating samples were coated with a very thin layer of carbon. The carbon conducts electricity which allows a good, sharp SEM image of the insulating sample to be obtained. Sometimes gold coatings are used. On this occasion I was being trained to use the (ancient but reliable) carbon coating machine. Always seem to be learning something new in my research work in engineering and recently via this project.

Creativity

Alison Beck

While pondering the question 'what is art?' I began to consider 'what is creativity?' or more importantly 'how do we generate creativity?' and how this links to the project.

I caught the end of a Horizon on BBC2, 'The Creative Brain: How Insight Works'. One suggestion made in the programme, was that creativity could be 'improved' by spending some time doing an engaging but not too demanding task (e.g. sorting Lego bricks into colours or simply going for a walk) which reduces activity in the frontal lobe of the brain (which apparently helps with creativity). This links to the suggestion of a 'walk around Furnace Park' in one of Hester's posts.

Some of the research activities I do in engineering are also 'engaging but not too demanding' tasks, I like to hope that this provides an opportuity and sets the scene for increased creativity! However, I still find walking the best activity for thinking and creativity. What do you find conducive to ideas generation? Clearly, there are many routes. The photographs and reports about the different work spaces, labs, workshops, and studios of the researchers and artists, illustrate that those visits are also great catalysts for creativity. I'm happy to show artists/researchers around my department, labs and so on and am keen to see other's workspaces!

Representation through language

Sarah Spencer

Bob recommended an art event linked to language and meaning at Site Gallery. The artist Anna Barham discussed her six-week residency in Sheffield and the relationship with the invited speakers, many of whom were locally based academics. The event was about language and its arbitrary nature, the non-referential symbolism of English phonemes and alphabet.

The artist worked in conversation with academics and I was intrigued to hear her thoughts about the process. Anna described how she needed time away from the academic discourses she'd been exposed to in order to 'look at it from the corner of her eye'. Anna explained that the aim of the residency was not to increase her understanding of literary and linguistic theory, nor was it her role to illustrate known theories, but to create anew, in a different mode.

This event made me think of our own academic/artistic conversations. All contributors find themselves confronting the boundaries between academic and artistic production, each bringing a unique perspective to that division. I wonder if we find ourselves looking through the corners of our eyes at each other's ideas and positions?

The discussion also covered Anna's work on anagrams as a route to pursuing meaning that isn't there. Elvis Presley: Silvery Sleeps. Furnace Park: recap far Kun. The interest is in the gaps, the spaces where we persistently search for meaning. It is in this space between meanings (or perhaps in representations?) where something lies. I wonder about the process of collaboration within this project: the cognitive process of making links and networks, finding cohesion. Is this space and absence—the gaps between our agendas—actually where the real meanings lie for us?

Reply 1: Jonathan Paragreen

Hi Sarah, your post reminds me a little bit of a conversation I had last week. I was in San Sebastian and was chatting with colleagues about language, especially what the Spanish call 'false gifts' in learning English. This is when an English word is similar in form to a Spanish word, but the meaning is completely different. In our meeting the following example came up: 'bomberos' meaning firefighter, and not bomb. I think we could find loads of examples of humans reading meaning into things when there is none: tea leaves, faces in the moon, cloud formations. I do wonder if it is natural that any gap will be filled with something. Buddleia plants do a great job of filling any industrial waste land.

Alison Beck

When I saw these tree roots at Yorkshire Sculpture Park last weekend, I was reminded of the description of the GPR survey to provide a visual representation of the subsurface 'tree roots and vegetation can sometimes effect the results'. The path is covered in exposed tree roots but the ones in the photo are cast in bronze (Hemali Bhuta connects deep roots of history with speed breakers).

Sea, sand and a whole variety of surfaces

Jonathan Paragreen

Just returned from a week long holiday in Anglesey. We set off the day after our picnic in Furnace Park, which remained at the forefront of my mind.

Whilst away we spent a lot of the week exploring the beaches and quite a bit walking, which gave me time to reflect on our topic of surfaces and relating it to the world around me. I reflected a lot on the materials which made up the various footpaths that we walked upon. And was surprised when I really started to think about the huge variety, in some places walking on soft sand paths which were really quite hard going, other places harder sand paths, some stone chipping paths, pebbles, stones laid to create a path; on one island a white path was completely made up of small shells. Some paths were dry and peaty which gave a nice hollow feel and sound as you walked upon them,

whilst compacted mud paths gave no such response. The surface of the rocks contained a huge variety of life, limpets and seaweed in abundance.

What struck me was the variety in a single subcategory of surface, such as sand. I walked along the beach towards the sea with my eyes shut (guided by my wife), just feeling the texture of the beach through my shoes. The differences I felt in a short stretch were amazing: from the soft sand with occasional tussocks of grass, into just soft sand, then into a harder damp sand, in places perfectly flat and in others with deep ripples. On the path to the sea you could hear shells being crushed underneath your shoes over pebbles. The different seaweeds were also evident, from the soft stringy type to a seaweed with pods which you could hear popping as you trod on them.

My thoughts also revolved around destruction and humans leaving their mark. At our picnic we looked at the litter in Furnace Park and thought about how it told a story of what the site has been used for: cans and used condoms, implying the activities carried out. But as I walking along the beaches and eroded footpaths I realised that I was quite literally leaving my own footprint on the landscape.

Alongside them and others you could identify the activities carried out: seeing prints from dogs, written messages in the sand, sand castles, or shallows where someone had sat or lay down. You could tell whether people were walking barefoot or in shoes or in walking boots, all in itself a record.

Perhaps most striking was a scene, which I thought was one of the most impressive sights of the holiday, but it was also where the most destruction of the surface had taken place. This was an old copper mine cut into a large hill. The landscape of rock was an amazing array of colours from reds and oranges, though to purples and greens and the scale of the site left me in awe. How can such man-made destruction finally become a thing of beauty, what phases of public opinion did it go through? From an ugly industrial site to a tourist attraction and apparently now used as a film set. Finally I thought that this was analogous to Furnace Park: is it currently towards the end of its ugly phase and about to be recognised as a place of interest and beauty?

A photo of the cleared site, taken on my cycle ride home from work on 25th July 2013. Looking at it in this cleared state, it seems very bare, almost a different place to where we researchers spent many happy hours with the artists. I expect that further changes will happen over the next few months. I think that this feeling of loss fits very well with many of our conversations on this blog; nothing stays the same forever and to create something new, something else must also be lost.

RIP the over-grown, rubbish strewn Furnace Park, although not universally loved, you had your supporters who appreciated you for what you were. We enjoyed your stories told by the litter and marks on your landscape. Although you are gone you will live on in the hearts and minds of those who have come to know you.

Participants

1 Dr Alison Beck

Alison worked in industry before attending the University of Sheffield to study chemistry as a mature student. She was awarded a PhD for research using plasmas to coat materials and modify their surface properties. She is an expert in analytical, spectroscopic and other techniques that help to improve our understanding of materials. These have been applied in academic research on carbon fibre composites and biomaterials for cell cultures as well as industrial projects such as improving adhesion in gas pipelines and the development of wigs.

2 Dr Mathew Cheeseman

Matthew works between English Literature, Folklore, Creative Writing, Music and Education. Recently he has focused on integrating artistic practice with interdisciplinary research.

3 Dr Caroline Evans

Caroline's research training in cell biology and biochemistry informs her current work in chemical engineering on medical and medical related projects. This is based at the ChELSI Institute (Chemical Engineering Life Science Interface), a multidisciplinary environment (chemical engineering, molecular biology, biochemistry, bioinformatics) which includes the newly established Sheffield Advanced Biomanufacturing Centre.

4 Bob Levene

Bob is an artist based in Sheffield. Her practice manifests as video and sound works, walks, performances, drawings and photography, often adopting psuedo-scientific approaches to explore the systems, tools and stories we live by and how they shape the way we see the world. She has shown work at ICA (London), Arnolfini (Bristol), Northern Gallery of Contemporary Art (Sunderland), Dundee Contemporary Art, Cornerhouse (Manchester), National Media Museum (Bradford), Kiasma Museum of Contemporary Art (Helsinki) and Yorkshire Sculpture Park (Wakefield).

5 Dr Jonathan Paragreen

Jonathan has a BEng-MEng degree in Chemical Engineering from the University of Bradford and a PhD in polymer rheology and extrusion modelling. He has worked in a variety of industries: bulk chemicals, oil and gas, aerospace, fuel cells and rail transport. Jonathan is a Research Associate at the University of Sheffield. Funded by EU FP7 grants, he works on rail transport security, whole life cycle and cost benefit analysis.

6 Hester Reeve

Hester Reeve is a multi-disciplinary artist. Her work has been shown in various venues including the former Randolph Street Gallery (Chicago), LIVE Biennale (Vancouver), Arnolfini (Bristol) and Tate Britain (London) as part of the Emily Davison Lodge. She is also a trained facilitator of David Bohm's Dialogue. Hester has a BA in Fine Art (Newcastle Polytechnic) and an MA in Philosophy, Values and the Environment (Lancaster University) and is currently Senior Lecturer in Fine Art at Sheffield Hallam University.

7 Dr Arne Schröder

Arne obtained an MSc in Biology at the University of Freiburg and a PhD in Ecology from Umeå University. He has worked in research at the University of Leeds and the University of Sheffield. He is now at the Leibniz Institute for Freshwater Ecology and Inland Fisheries (IGB) in Berlin. His private interests range from the philosophy of science to human history. As an ecologist his work is concerned with why we see a certain amount of animals or plants at a given time at a given place.

8 Dr Sarah Spencer

Sarah is a lecturer in Human Communication Sciences. She has previously worked for the charity ICAN on projects in secondary schools and the youth justice system, Newcastle University on a project developing evidence-based approaches to communication supporting classrooms and the NHS in Sunderland and Middlesbrough as a speech and language therapist with children. She researches adolescent language in contexts of social disadvantage using both qualitative and quantitative methods.

9 HAND

HAND is a multi-disciplinary design company, made up of Alasdair Hiscock and Ben Dunmore. With roots in fanzine publishing, the pair have gone to work on an array of projects from art books to lighting installations, web design to clothing.

First Meeting

01/02/2013
Furnace Park
The participants met each other in advance of the group blog.

Sandpit Studio

08/04/2013
Humanities Research Institute
The participants decided to continue the collaborative process instead of nominating an artist to make work in Furnace Park.

Picnic

17/05/2013
Furnace Park

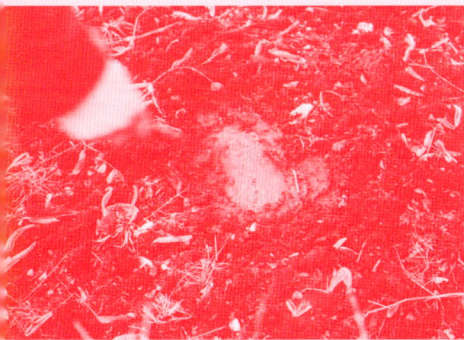

These are some photos of our visit to Furnace Park (thanks to Ivan and Katya for access and for providing chairs). We had a picnic, some lovely soup, scones with jam and cream, cherry cake and plenty of tea! We also took the chance to explore and discuss the project more. We discussed themes that had emerged from the blog, and agreed to meet again to each investigate/interpret the concept of ground as an extension or continuation of the theme of surface. What next?

It was interesting to reflect on Sarah's blog, discussing an artist in residence for a linguistic project, where the artist Anna explained that the aim of the residency was not to increase her understanding of literary and linguistic theory nor was it her role to illustrate known theories, but to create anew and in a different mode.

1. Structure
2. Reflection
3. Cementation works
4. A space for ants
5. Investigating
6. The meeting space

A Proposal From The Artists To The Researchers

The Work:

A curated dinner party under the open sky in the park for invited guests to serve up the book (literally, as one of the courses).

The Thinking Behind The Work:

We wanted to build on the spirit of the project so far and maintain it in the final work.

We wanted to integrate the book into a creative event rather than have it 'on display.'

We wanted to have continuity between the project process and the end result.

We wanted to share and celebrate the process, dialogue and interdisciplinarity with the public (in particular people living and working in the furnace park area), colleagues and stakeholders.

We wanted to propose a framework where everyone participating has the space to contribute something on their own terms.

How It Will Work:

Each researcher and artist will invite a select amount of guests.

Printed invitations will be presented by hand.

Researchers and artists will work together onsite to cook a 5 course meal for the guests (this is about spending time together working/chatting in the park and producing something for other people to enjoy, so no stressing over complex menus etc.)

The event will be held together by a toastmaster (we will hire one).

Guests will arrive at the park and be welcomed by the toastmaster, encouraged to explore the park by the offer of h'orderves served by waiters (student volunteers) hidden around the park.

The researchers and artists act as hosts.

The toast master calls the guests to the beautiful (and uniquely) laid table:

A toast* is made.

The first course is served (Starters)

A toast* is made.

The second course is served (The Book)

A toast* is made.

The third course is served (Mains)

A toast* is made.

The fourth course is served (Dessert)

A toast* is made.

The fifth course is served (Coffee)

The Details:

The toast* is a chance for the artists and researchers and invited guests to say something, read something or do something. We will bring back the megaphone. It should be short and in some way connect to the experience and spirit of the project. It could be a reading from the book, a description of an aspect you liked, and action that points out your favourite bit of the park, a description of something you want to go on to do and so on... the limit is your imagination.

~~We~~ ~~we will~~ and make small interventions that will contribute to the overall aesthetic and design of the table set up. We aim to design a special napkin, for example. We will use a table cloth, china plates, glasses etc. Although the event will be formal the feel will be one of DIY, so no gold 'wedding' chairs will be in sight!

The meal will be served by waiters (students dressed up in black and white).

Food will be simple, wholesome and manageable for us to cook and serve. But we want to really put people through the process of a proper meal with wine and all the '"unwinding" and "getting to know you" and "after dinner stories" that a dinner party invites. I.e We want people to feel part of the special event rather than feel visitors or spectators.

Think special, fun, real and DIY rather than fancy. That is... apart from the clothes. Dress Up.

Documentation:

The event will be documented (mainly through stills photography but video of the toasts) but we plan for this to be done at a distance and partially obscured so that no one feels self-conscious.

A guest book will be available after the meal for guests to leave their feedback – another form of documentation.

What to think about:

What to toast?
Who to invite/how many can we accommodate?
What food to cook?
Does anyone know a suitable, efficient events organiser?

See you on Friday 26th July to discuss and develop this together!

24/07/2014
Email
Re: From The Toast Master General, a proposal from the artists to the researchers. A result of a meeting between Bob and Hester.

Ground
Investigations

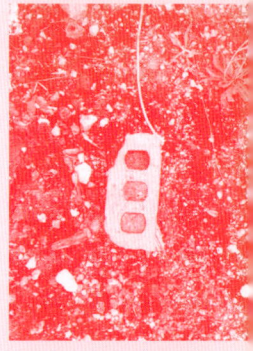

01/07/2013
Furnace Park
A research/play day for all the participants.

Group Meeting

Changes to Furnace Park

Tim's control box—possibility now gone.
Hole filled in with concrete?
BL: Have to be very clear—exactly what is going to be in the Park on Sep 29th. BL and HR to confirm with ACJ.
HR: Bleak, stark park will leave a strong visual impression.
JP: Emotional response to the wasteground. Sad to see it go.

What of the proposal?

JP: Tempted to say a eulogy for what was.
HR: Emotional connection to the creative process too.
MJC: Day-glo spots everywhere.
BL: Hazard tape?
HR: Smoke machine?
HR: Engagement with the local public. Don't need to do a song and dance. Symbolic of engagement and interdisciplinaratry.
BL: How do we resolve this? Democratic process. Dialogue from day one. Didn't want to plonk on some art at the end that was detached. Structure to contribute.
CE: Nice to be given equal space.
MJC: Elitism challenge.
AB: Agreed, need to be careful.
BL and HR: Agree to make the meal open to the public with targeted invites.
BL: Doesn't resolve how it's going to be perceived. Perceptions of elitism. Community participatory art challenge—flying in, having an event and flying out. So to come in and invite a whole lot of local people and go away is worse.

SS: Is it?
HR: Tired about liberal agendas—'respecting the funders'. Tired of hearing academics and artists.
SS: Locals would feel a little bit on the spot.
BL: Elitism—one of the purposes of the dinner party is the book launch. Locals to be part of the book launch. Meeting a problem.
HR: Academics having the nice meal—whose cooking that meal?
MJC: Should be open in some way. Question here about audience and participation.
HR: If this was major Tate Britain show—that would be a big issue. But it is not. Flyers locally... Open call? Poster on the site—billboard advertising the event.
CE: Checking the emails coming in from the thing.
BL and HR: Hand-write a flyer.
SS: Read spirit of it—didn't think of elitism. It didn't feel like that. Agree—challenging perceptions.

The book

BD: Can you eat the book?
BL: Can we have something on the front cover that you tear off
BD: Put it in a crisp packet and then open it... Sandwich bag... salad bags, tin foil—roll up a magazine. Rubbish—fits in with all the rubbish.
AH: 124 page A5 decided.
HR: One thing our project does is document Furnace Park.
AH: Book/magazine hybrid. Read back to back. Different voices, different streams of thought. Split it 40 each between blog/contributions/events.
BD: Organised around hidden themes. Interviews not good. Write what you know about.

Five themes:
1. Art/Science, Art/Research, Identity. Learning from each other, finding how similar the processes were. Lots of blogs around this.
2. Surface. What can surface tells us? What's beyond the surface?
3. The site. What is this place, here, temporality, permanence, emotion, ground.
4. Engaging the public/Politics/Politics-economic-social. What is the public, why should they be interested? Find a local?
5. Dialogue/Method. Collaboration, practice, benefits, how does it work. Not artist into the department as court painter. ISBN numbers? BL to find out.
BD: Chronology. Annotation. Timeline?
Glossary of terms. BD and AH to do. Others to be commissioned.
Friday 30th August deadline for contributions—everyone.
Friday 2nd August deadline for sharing photos AH to set up Dropbox.

Logistics for meal

80 people.
13 FP people.
Personal invite and an interesting invite each.
Continued dialogue.
JR to begin document Google Docs, everyone to add wishlist for Friday 2nd August.

26/07/2013
G03 Jessop West
Minutes from group meeting.

Breakfast
Toasts

29/08/2013
Furnace Park
A breakfast held in lieu of the dinner party. All the
participants gave toasts.

Hester Reeve

Perhaps it is fitting that circumstances forced us into a private breakfast celebration of our book rather than a public evening meal. After dinner speeches fall into recognized social conventions whereas 'after breakfast speeches' smacks of poetic shenanigans! We sit around this table as 'creative agents'. I am deliberately avoiding the arts-science dichotomy here; I think this whole thing worked because somehow we ignited the capacity to be creative agents in one another. Don't underestimate that as a result. So, I raise my coffee cup up to each and every one of you: it's been great!

I also raise my coffee cup up to our avoiding any resolution of our project in terms of a public artwork, or any piece of art per se. We were all thrown out into the open here in Furnace Park and it kind of worked. A process evolved of itself that had less to do with art or science, and more to do with just delighting in spending time with one another exploring this unprescribed piece of wasteland. Perhaps we became as unruly as the park itself, and this is why Manet's 'shocking' painting Le Déjeuner sur l'herbe of 1862 comes to mind. This project unwittingly facilitated 'authorized' breaks from the everyday beaurocratic rigors and repressions of our academic professions. Is it any wonder that our behavior was that of wild spirits chasing their tails in the playground? Like the primitive ideal of the first parks founded in the country, Furnace Park has allowed us to escape the norms of the city and, perhaps more importantly, the norms of academia. We didn't come together with a shared problem or aim, we were thrown together with the park the only common thing between us. But what if it is in the very aspect of meeting and eating together in the park that we have founded something? Like today, is this a breakfast or is this a protest? We deliberately came here at the crack of dawn, cooked food and laid our table out in Furnace Park: aren't we symbolically activating the commons?

On reflection, working with you all here has reminded me of an experience of Admirals Park in Essex where I spent my childhood. My most powerful and 'forget everything else, the world is potential' memory of that park was when my sister, a few friends and myself formed the MCC (the Metal Collecting Club). We had been paddling a quite unremarkable stream and discovered an old rusty bar, about three meters long. It fascinated us for not only was it a foreign body but we had discovered it right in the middle of everything normal. Once disturbed and in our hands, the world changed. We did not transfigure the rod into an alien spacecraft or Native American spear—it stayed a rusty rod. It was we who changed ourselves and the possibilities of what could be done, or, rather, how one could be done by the world! From then on out, we spent our days gathering as much rusty metal from the stream as we could. We didn't make anything with it, but I did make a special notebook to record all the different shapes we had found and that was extremely satisfying.

I think it was the unprogrammed play where one has to invent from ground zero that was so generative for me as a child, and it has been a similar process working with all of you. Quite probably as artists and scientists we don't get enough of this unfettered creative almost aimless space. Well, it's not as if we didn't discuss a lot of really interesting concerns and ideas, but what sort of won over was not any of those ideas but a sense of being inspired by being together in the park.

So, I raise my glass.

Caroline Evans
This speech is going to be a mix: from some notes that I made earlier and some talking as I go. While thinking about what to say, I was inspired by Matt saying the project could allow us to 'reimagine ourselves'. That really speaks to the sense of possibility that I have experienced through this project.

Initially, I was very uncertain about what was expected of researchers and what was expected of artists. But I wanted to do it, and what struck me throughout the process was the mutual respect shown by both. As the project has progressed, these groupings seem more and more arbitrary. I liked too how we moved forward, very much together. On this point, thanks to Matt for his excellent project running and ensuring not only that we kept to the meeting time length, but also that we made decisions, met deliverables by moving lots of discussion and debate into action. I also really appreciate the friendship that developed, for example, after the ground investigation we all moved to a café for review of the afternoon and then spontaneously to the pub to spend continued time together. New working relationships and friendships have been a welcome outcome of the project. It's great that Bob Levene is now Artist in Residence in Engineering at Sheffield and that Alison, Jonathan and I can continue to collaborate in this framework.

In terms of the reimagining, I never considered myself a writer (other than of academic reports, articles, grants) and I found the blog an unfamiliar, challenging format, but seeing and contributing to the themes emerging was a really unique process. Later in the project, it was decided that we (whether artist or researcher by training) would each create material for the book. This decision was challenging—daunting even—but it was exciting to go with that idea too and see where it ended up.

My 'piece' for the book is a work in progress, but essentially the basic idea is to draw a circle on a map around Furnace Park and then investigate the industrial heritage within. This isn't aimed at being researched before setting off, more of a walk around to see what is readily apparent and I am writing an explanation to accompany it. And when I set off from my department, late one summer afternoon, camera in hand, it was with a real sense of excitement at the adventure of it all.

So what you all have given me is the courage to do something radically different in style and approach.

And my toast is 'thank you and to us'.

Sarah Spencer
This project resulted in researchers, artists, academics, doctors, professionals and practitioners becoming creators of photos, friendships, new understandings, perspectives, blogs and words. We were brought together because of our very different viewpoints, skills and methods. We were brought together to share a fresh artist-academic collaboration with the public. Our wealth brought us together; employment statuses, reputations, outputs. Yet in Furnace Park none of this had exchange or use value.

We were all observers watching ants and finches and holes, discomfort and uncertainty, small discoveries and boundaries, procedures and expectations. Observing a small patch of land change from a forgotten trace of industry amid the traffic, a large financial office and the sex trade into a site of health, safety, possibility. Along the way, we all compartmentalised the experience as fun, something different, trivialising Furnace Park against our usual business. This fun and lightness belied a firm grounding. Furnace Park grounded us. The earth, the cement, the cracks and the debris. Our specialisms half understood whispers. Carefully negotiated respect glimpsed through hazy notions of what we do and who we are, where our values lie.

We listened to each other and our boundaries loosened. Furnace Park grounded us like a walk outdoors near our home, like being lost, grounded us like friends' company, like a good book, like yoga and Atticus Finch. Ground: it took us to brown, grey, circle, concrete, earth level, level under. To horizons and soil and substance and diameters, shapes, tea, smoke, continuous points.

The ground offered new understanding, careful quiet observation, a complete rejection of all research that went before. While in our hot bubbling furnace we met grand societal challenges, impact, engagement, money, entitlement and added value, for a few moments Furnace Park was just ground and an absence of position and discipline. The value of this, beyond subversive art therapy,

is hard to articulate. It lies in the absences, lies in the creative stretch between our experiences. The shifted sense of what we are in relation to knowing, researching, observing

Jonathan Paragreen

This is ad lib. I will try to keep it fairly brief. I just wanted to say that I have thoroughly enjoyed working on this project. I am quite a self-conscious person, but when early on I looked at Bob and Hester's work online, it was obvious that anything goes. And for me I think that has been one of the great aspects of the project: to feel comfortable in doing whatever you want to do.

Much of this comfort is also due to this being a great group of people; Hester and Bob have been fantastically enthusiastic and encouraging to us researchers. I feel that throughout the work I have really got to know everyone. In previous workplaces I have found that you can work with someone for years without really getting to know them, but here everyone has really committed to the project and put a part of themselves into the activities we have carried out and as a result I feel much closer to you all.

So I would like to raise a toast to us!

Alison Beck

I haven't prepared any notes for this speech... Throughout the project, in the writings and blog, I have noticed how clearly everyone's own distinct voice shone through. In our everyday work so often, we are constrained by style, what should be said, and how it should be said. This also happened to me in a different way regarding the spoken voice. When I first arrived in Sheffield, people could not understand my Derbyshire accent and so that had to change quite a bit! I think the work we have done together in this project has somehow freed us up, helped us learn about different ways of working and thinking and also allowed all of our voices to come across more clearly.

I wanted to wear something special for our breakfast, so I'll say a bit about the cape I am wearing. A lot of you know that I like making things from textiles and sewing things, and the cape was something simple and fun. I made it from some fabric that I had printed up (as a fabric poster) with the microscopic images I took of people's clothes during our day of Ground Investigations at Furnace Park. Let me point out a few of the images (you're are all on it!): Matt's belt, Sarah's necklace, Caroline's ring, Hester's tattoo, Jonathan's ring, Bob's bracelet and quite a few others with Furnace Park as the background.

The toast: to you all; it's been great!

Arne Schröder

When we started, I was completely lost. But I think I'm not anymore. The whole thing has been a process, for me a journey, that let me discover a lot of new things that I never really thought about. Working with Bob and Hester, I'd never worked with artists before, the discussions we had at the Union or at our meetings was really helpful to give me an understanding of what you can do when you do not have your narrow-minded scientific view (which I'm very proud of) approach to the

world. And I think that's one lasting effect, one lasting thing for me from this whole project. And I'm really glad that I've done it, I've met you guys. I had a lot of fun and I also discovered that it's not about producing something because that's what I think I had a little bit in mind that in the end there would be some sculpture. You know my posts about sculpting things and stuff like that, there would be a sculpture now or an art project. Because I thought that's what artists do, they put something there. And Bob your work about walking around Sheffield city borders gave me a way to appreciate the process not the end product, but the process. Which in a way is quite fitting because as scientists we are also usually looking at processes not only at the end product, at least for me as an ecologist. You have a lot of processes that shape constantly an eco-system. It's dynamic, it's going on, it's going somewhere, it's not static. And I think this matched the processes in this project here. Yeah, I really enjoyed it. I want to thank you guys, it was fun.

Cheers!

Matthew Cheeseman
I'd like to raise a toast to:

—Dr Guillaume Hautbergue
—Dr Helen Moggridge
—Dr Tom Stafford (and to his daughter)
—Tim Lewis (and to his son)

All of whom would be here save for time.
Now for those who devoted more time than they expected to give, in an environment which eats your time, consumes it. Somehow they managed to feed themselves on a notion of artistic practice. I toast:

Alison, for her ferocious creativity and superhero cape, Jonathan, for his pleasure through innovative deviation, Arne, for his dignity in descent, Caroline, for her searching attention and calm persistence, Sarah, for her soulful intellect and driving conscience, Ben, for his welcome cynicism and paper stock enthusiasm, Alasdair, for his savage humour and steady hand, Hester, for her effervescent philosophy, a combination of air and stone, Bob, for her tenacious vision, water and earth.

And finally Gemma, for being here, and letting us imagine the public through her camera.

Bob Levene
It's lovely to hear such heartfelt toasts from all, they all seemed to resonate with each other.

I'd also like to acknowledge the 'gentle witnessing' by those who haven't been involved in the project: Gemma Thorpe taking the photographs and Joe Moore doing the gardening.

Carl Jung said there were four ways of knowing: feeling, intuition, sensing as well as thinking.

In our world, so much value is placed on what we can measure and put a number to, as well as the act of measuring itself, but from what I've just heard it's the inbetween, the without reason, the connectedness, the ground, the small and a sense of that has shined through.

The wasteland offered space to re-imagine, the kindness, respect and openness of the participants created a safe environment, which for some 'gave courage to do something radically different'. Surely these are the conditions for real change, new perspectives, new collaborations? With the unspoken principles of play, empathy and listening we all got to place value on the unspoken, un-ended, the process, the relationships and sharing rather than the objects, measured, resolved.

So a toast, to you all.

This
Really
Happened

No Picnic: Explorations In Art and Research
Furnace Park, 27th May, 2014, 11am–2.30pm

To launch our book, NO PICNIC, we're holding a picnic. The book presents what happened when research-ers and artists explored each other's work in Furnace Park, which was, when we started, a wasteland.

The participants incorporated artistic practices in their research techniques, often alongside events in the wasteland. The project addressed the approaches we take individually and collectively within art, science and investigation. All of this is documented in our book.

Ideally we'd like you to comment on our explorations with insights from your own work and thoughts in this area. We want the event to build on these comments to ask, ultimately, what is research, how should it be carried out, and how should a university involve the wider community in these activities? Your comments will stimulate this discussion, and of course there will be a picnic provided.

Furnace Park is in Shalesmoor, a ten minute walk from the University of Sheffield. We'd like to begin the picnic at 11am and end at 2.30pm with some music. Would you let me know as soon as possible whether you'd be able to make it? Please Reply by Wednesday 16th April at the latest.

Finally, do you know anyone else who would be suitable to speak?

Thanks!

Matt Cheeseman
Sarah Spencer
Bob Levene
Hester Reeve
Alison Beck
Jonathan Paragreen
Caroline Evans
Arne Schröder

28/02/2014
Email
Book launch planning.